HUNGER CHANGES EVERYTHING

Hunger Changes Everything
Seeking the Face of God

Jessica Seetaram

Without limiting the rights under copyright(s) reserved below, no part of this publication may be reproduced, stored in, or introduced into a retrieval system, or transmitted in any form or by any means (electronic, mechanical, photocopying, recording, or otherwise) without the prior permission of the publisher and the copyright owner.

The content of this book is provided "AS IS." The publisher and the author make no guarantees or warranties as to the accuracy, adequacy, completeness of, or results to be obtained from using the content of this book, including any information that can be accessed through hyperlinks or otherwise, and expressly disclaim any warranty expressed or implied, including but not limited to implied warranties of merchantability or fitness for a particular purpose. This limitation of liability shall apply to any claim or cause whatsoever, whether such claim or cause arises in contract, tort, or otherwise. In short, you, the reader, are responsible for your choices and the results they bring.

The scanning, uploading, and distributing of this book via the internet or any other means without the permission of the publisher and copyright owner is illegal and punishable by law. Please purchase only authorized copies and do not participate in or encourage piracy of copyrighted materials. Your support of the author's rights is appreciated.

Scripture quotations without attribution are from the King James Version of the Bible, which is public domain.

Scripture quotations marked (NLT) are taken from the Holy Bible, New Living Translation, copyright © 1996, 2004, 2015 by Tyndale House Foundation. Used by permission of Tyndale House Publishers, Inc., Carol Stream, Illinois 60188. All rights reserved.

Copyright © 2025 by Jessica J. Seetaram. All rights reserved.

Released February 2025
ISBN: 978-1-64457-785-1 (PB)
ISBN: 978-1-64457-788-2 (HC)

Rise UP Publications
644 Shrewsbury Commons Ave
Ste 249
Shrewsbury PA 17361
United States of America

www.riseUPpublications.com
Phone: 866-846-5123

DEDICATED TO...

the one who saved and called me His own, My Lord and Savior Jesus Christ—

to you I owe my life.

~AND~

My loving parents, who have gone on to their heavenly home, James and Matiranie (Mary) Seetaram—

you will forever be in my heart

You were born with a God-given purpose. Do not leave this world until you have attained all that God has in store for you. Let your hunger and desperation for Him propel you into your destiny.

"They that hunger and thirst after righteousness, shall be filled."

CONTENTS

Introduction 11

Chapter 1 15
The Early Days

Chapter 2 21
The Teenage Years—Salvation

Chapter 3 27
Teenage Years and 1978

Chapter 4 41
Crossing The Atlantic—Welcome to America The Beautiful

Chapter 5 45
The Early Days of Ministry in New York

Chapter 6 49
I Shall Not Die Before My Time

Chapter 7 57
A Place of Spiritual Discontent

Chapter 8 61
Y2k—My Greatest Victory Won – Desperation Leads to Transformation

Chapter 9 71
To Walk on Water, You Must Step Out of the Boat

Chapter 10 79
Deep Calleth to Deep

Chapter 11 87
The Tide Is Turning

Chapter 12 95
Back Into the Unknown

Chapter 13 101
Crossing The East River

Chapter 14 109
Restoration of the Call

Chapter 15 117
The Evangelist

Chapter 16 121
What No Eye Has Seen

Chapter 17   129
Live A Life Of Purpose

Chapter 18   137
Finally—It's Not Finished Yet

Afterword   143
About the Author   145

INTRODUCTION

> For I know the thoughts that I think toward you, saith the Lord, thoughts of peace, and not of evil, to give you an expected end.
>
> —JEREMIAH 29:11

For every person born into this world, God has a plan for their life.

> Before I formed thee in the belly I knew thee; and before thou camest forth out of the womb I sanctified thee, and I ordained thee a prophet unto the nations.
>
> —JEREMIAH 1:5

Many people will live and die and never fulfill the plans that God has for them. God never changes His mind. His Word will stand forever, and His plans will always be available to those who seek after Him.

INTRODUCTION

> For the gifts and the calling of God are irrevocable
> [for He does not withdraw what He has given, nor
> does He change His mind about those to whom
> He gives His grace or to whom He sends His call].
>
> — ROMANS 11:29(AMP)

Whether you are young or old, it's not too late to fulfill your calling and destiny. God is not bound or restricted by age or any circumstance of man. Your education will not hinder God. Your family situation will not affect Him. Your financial situation does not matter to Him. The family you were born into cannot change His plans for you. It is all up to you!

Where you are now is not where you will be in the future. You may be in ministry and faithfully serving the Lord, but inside of you, there is more. You feel it but cannot put your hands on it. You are unsatisfied with your life and desperately desire some change. It's not money or material things—you have all that. But it seems something is missing; there must be more to life than this.

The key is in Matthew 6:33, *"But seek ye first the kingdom of God, and his righteousness; and all these things shall be added unto you."* It means putting God first in your life, making Him your primary concern, and He will take care of all that concerns you. This was the verse that the Holy Spirit used to explode this revelation in my heart. I was never the same. After reading this verse and memorizing it as a child, it finally spoke to me loud and clear. This revelation that all I needed to do was "Make God #1 in my life, put Him first in everything, and the rest is up to Him" blew me away and overwhelmed me. So, I put everything in God's hands and decided to do what the Psalmist David did: I began to "run hard" after God.

INTRODUCTION

> My soul followeth hard after thee: thy right hand upholdeth me.
>
> — PSALM 63:8

I used to think like many of you who love the Lord and are serving Him faithfully. You see others in ministry and think they are "special," and that is not for you. You are okay with serving the Lord, teaching kids, or being a greeter. You cannot see yourself having your own ministry or going higher or further because you do not have the ability, education, or background. God expects us to keep moving, going higher, deeper, and accomplishing more. We are meant to keep going from glory to glory and not remain the same.

In 2 Corinthians 3:18, the Bible says, *"But we all, with open face beholding as in a glass the glory of the Lord, are changed into the same image from glory to glory, even as by the Spirit of the Lord."*

When the Lord calls us, and we answer Him and obey His call, He will equip us with all we need to accomplish the task. It's never based on what we have, who we are, where we came from, or our abilities. The work of the Lord is accomplished only by Him through the Holy Spirit, who empowers us. Never forget this: it's *"Not by might, nor by power, but by my Spirit, saith the Lord of hosts"* (Zechariah 4:6). If you keep this verse of Scripture in the forefront of your mind, you will never worry about who you are or what you can accomplish because it will all be about Him, for Him, and through Him. This will ease all the burdens of ministry for you. Amen!

The purpose of this book is to ignite a fire in you, motivating you not to settle for the "status quo." If you are desperate, hungry, and thirsty for more of God and want to see your life be all that you were created to be in this world, then join me on this adventure that will change your life forever!

CHAPTER 1
THE EARLY DAYS

One of the most famous Bible verses in all the world is John 3:16, *"For God so loved the world, that he gave his only begotten Son, that whosoever believeth in him should not perish, but have everlasting life."* This is the gospel in one verse. I am thankful that when I did not know God, He loved me and sought me out.

> ... there is none that seeketh after God.
>
> — ROMANS 3:11

> No man can come to me, except the Father which hath sent me draw him: and I will raise him up at the last day.
>
> —JOHN 6:44

It is God who pursues the heart of man, not the other way around. It was clearly the Lord who pursued me. I did not grow up in a Christian home. I knew very little of the Bible. So, I credit my salvation totally to the Lord's doing, and it is marvelous in my eyes. Like the believers in Acts 19:2, I never heard that there is a Holy Ghost. I was lost and going to Hell, but the Lord intercepted my life at an early age and saved me.

At the age of six to ten years old, I tagged along with one of my older sisters to a Seventh-day Adventist church. To this day, I don't recall even one sermon the pastor preached, but what has left a lifelong imprint on my heart, mind, and soul were the hymns they sang. From then to now, I still love and sing the hymns. It saddens me that many churches no longer sing the hymns or have hymn books. The words of the hymns are based on the Scriptures and carry a clear message from the gospel. My sister got married when I was ten and moved away. I no longer had anyone to take me to church, so my church life and attendance ended!

In the meantime, the enemy was trying to hook me into another religion—Hinduism—but God had a plan for my life. About a year later, the Assemblies of God began an outreach in the small Dutch village called Parika, where we lived. About five to six teenagers and young adults from Central Assembly of God in Georgetown would travel to my village every Sunday. They would then visit the homes in the area and invite the children to Sunday school. I was allowed to go. I never missed a Sunday. Sunday school was the first hour, followed by the Worship Service. Just when the Devil thought he had me, God, by His mighty right hand, made a way out of his trap and sent His word through this outreach. Hallelujah!

We met at a "Dance Hall." On Friday and Saturday nights, there were concerts with music, dancing, and alcohol. On Sunday morning, we would go early to clean up the beer bottles and cans to prepare the place for church. The benches we sat on had no back brace, and air conditioning was the open windows that allowed the breeze from the Atlantic Ocean to flow through. We never complained that we had to sit for over three hours; we were glad to be in church. *"Never despise the days of small beginnings"* (Zechariah 4:10), for in due season, God will increase you if you faint not.

In Sunday school, we learned the Word of God. I consumed every bit like a hungry child who hadn't eaten for days and believed every word like a little child. I am weeping as I write this sentence because this childlike faith has been the foundation of my walk with the Lord. I will talk more about this in Chapter 2. God's Word came to me like water in a desert place. Psalm 42:1 says, *"As the deer panteth for the water brooks, so panteth my soul after thee, O God."* I was hungry but did not know what would satisfy me. I was thirsty but did not know what could quench my thirst. I was desperate for something, some meaning in life, but I did not know where to find it. I had no knowledge of a spiritual life or that God was able to satisfy all the longing in my heart and soul.

Each Sunday during the Service, we sang and prayed, and one of our Sunday school teachers preached the Word. Mostly, the most senior person would preach. Every time altar calls were made, I raised my hand to receive Jesus Christ as my Lord and Savior. I must have raised my hand hundreds of times to receive Jesus Christ as my Lord and Savior. Now, I am sure many of you did the same, so don't act so spiritual. At the time, I didn't understand that confessing my sins with my mouth and believing in my heart would lead to my salvation. I did it every time the preacher asked if anyone would like to give their life to Christ and be born again. Remember, I am coming from a background with no semblance of Christ in my home. I had good, kind, religious people around me, but they were not Christians.

After a while of attending this outreach, I began to assist in the Children's Ministry, working with toddlers. I was about twelve years old by now. My good attendance, commitment to the Word, and the tasks assigned to me led to them asking me to lead worship for our services. I love to sing. I may not qualify for *American Idol*, but I will sing loud and strong for Jesus all the days of my life. Amen! Psalm 100:1 says, *"Make a joyful noise unto the Lord."* That's enough validation for me.

As my knowledge of the Word grew, so did my faith.

> So then faith cometh by hearing, and hearing by the word of God.
>
> — ROMANS 10:17

No one can become strong without the Word of God. Preaching and teaching the Word to a lost and dying world is important because that causes faith in a non-believer to become a believer in Christ. It also causes faith to grow stronger and stronger in the believer. The more of the Word we consume, eat, and digest, the stronger our faith will become.

There was no television or telephone where I grew up. Actually, we got electricity only a few years prior. After the teachers and leaders left on Sunday, we had no means of contacting them until the next Sunday. There was no way to call anyone for prayer or encouragement. You couldn't reach anyone to answer your questions or give counsel. I was about thirteen years old and took everything I learned in Sunday school and service very seriously. I began to pray and read the Word. I wanted to live for Christ and wanted my life to be pleasing to Him. The fear of God came upon me, and I did not want to miss the rapture, so I decided I had better live right every day.

Like every young child, whether youth or teenager, we look up to those around us who are older as role models. It could be a brother or sister in your home, family, community, or church. I remember how my life seemed to have no purpose, no joy, and no future. My Sunday school teachers and leaders all seemed to have purpose, joy, and happiness. So, I purposed in my heart that "I want to be just like them." They had something I did not have, and I wanted what they had. I wanted to be like them. We used to sing this song, "Sunday school, Sunday school, I love Sunday school. I love my superintendent, and I love my teachers too. When I grow to be a big, big girl, a teacher I will be, to teach the other boys and girls what my teacher taught to me." This is exactly what I wanted to do, and so it was. I taught Sunday school for twenty-four years, from toddlers to third grade, and then youths.

> Thou shalt also decree a thing, and it shall be established unto thee: and the light shall shine upon thy ways.
>
> —JOB 22:28

CHAPTER 2
THE TEENAGE YEARS—SALVATION

This was the happiest and most enjoyable season of my life. Getting to know the Bible and what God said about me began to give me hope and purpose. When I was fifteen years old, my Sunday school teacher paid for me to go to Youth Camp. I had never heard of Youth Camp before and did not know what to expect. My mom totally opposed it until my oldest brother begged her to let me go. She agreed but was not happy since "girl children" do not go away from home for any reason, not even for a day, much less a week in the jungle. She took so long to agree that I almost missed the ferry.

There were many teenage boys and girls at the camp. Like most Youth Camps, there were strict rules to follow. They assigned us duties in the kitchen to clean up and tidy up our beds. There were morning devotions where we had to get up early to spend time in God's Word and prayer. In the evening, there were Worship Services. Everyone gathered in the Fellowship Hall could feel the powerful presence of God. They sang new worship songs and choruses that I had never heard before. It seemed like I was in a different world. I had not seen that many people worshipping together before. It was beautiful. His presence was real.

Two songs stuck with me from that Youth Camp, and every time I hear them, the memories take me right back to the camp. One was 1 John 4:7-8, *"Beloved, let us love one another: for love is of God; and everyone that loveth is born of God, and knoweth God. He that loveth not knoweth not God; for God is love. So, beloved, let us love one another."* The other song was *"Heavenly Father I Appreciate You."* Whenever I hear this song (I don't hear it in churches anymore) on CD in my car or at some old-fashioned revival service, it brings tears to my eyes. It still speaks to me like it did then. It takes me back to that camp where He revealed Himself to me and called me into His ministry.

> And I thank Christ Jesus our Lord, who hath enabled me, for that he counted me faithful, putting me into the ministry.
>
> — 1 TIMOTHY 1:12

The last night of the camp was a "Grand Finale" service, which included a long altar call to receive Jesus as Savior and to receive the Baptism of the Holy Spirit. At this point, I did not know much about the Holy Spirit, but I wanted to get saved again so I wouldn't go to Hell. Something happened to me when I responded to the altar call. I prayed the prayer, repented of my sins, and gave my heart to Jesus. I felt something as the Holy Ghost touched me. I was weeping at the altar as I felt His hand on my life. When this service was over, I clearly felt the call of God to preach His Word. The experience changed me—it changed my heart, my mind, and my life. It was a complete transformation.

As we returned home, I was not the same. The fire of God burned in me for the lost. God gave me His heart for those in my community who did not know Him. A few weeks after the camp, I took to the street to "Preach" and do the work of an evangelist. The Holy Spirit gave me the boldness to preach. There was no fear of the Devil or anyone. I was a very shy person, but when it came to the gospel, I was as bold as a lion. The fact that I was now saved and going to Heaven made me want to prevent anyone from going to Hell. I preached all I knew about Hell, Heaven, salvation, the rapture, and how everyone needed to get saved before it was too late. I didn't know theology, but I knew Jesus came, died, rose again, went to Heaven, and is coming back. From the street, I targeted the homes of the Muslims since they were the hardest to come to Christ. I am thankful they never stoned me; today, it might be much different. Many of my school friends were Muslim, and when I went to their homes on Sunday mornings to invite them to Sunday school, their parents forbade them. This saddened me.

To reach more people, I went to the ferry terminal, where hundreds of people traveled every day. I felt the urgency to let people know that Jesus loves them and that He is coming back soon. In those days, preachers preached the fear of God into us, and it kept us living holy since Jesus could burst through the clouds and take His church away at any time. It did not matter that there was no music, singers, or microphone then—I simply preached His Word. All I had was my Bible and the Holy Spirit. It was all I needed. To this day, Zechariah 4:6 is at the forefront of my mind when it comes to ministry: *"Not by might, nor by power, but by my spirit, saith the Lord of hosts."* I have learned to trust the Holy Spirit and do all He asked of me.

While many of my classmates from school were pursuing boys, fashion, and the things of this world, I was pursuing God. In the Assemblies of God in those days, women did not wear pants, makeup, or jewelry. People considered this as being holy. The world called it "plain Jane." This is where my childlike faith comes in. Whatever I was told, I obeyed. I believed every word in the Bible literally—if it says gossip is wrong, I didn't do it. If stealing and lying are sins, I didn't do it. If coveting and disobedience are sins, I didn't do it. If fornication is a sin, I didn't do it. If smoking and drinking alcohol are sins, I didn't touch them. I learned that my body is the temple of God.

> What? know ye not that your body is the temple of
> the Holy Ghost which is in you, which ye have of
> God, and ye are not your own?
> For ye are bought with a price: therefore glorify God
> in your body, and in your spirit, which are God's.
>
> — 1 CORINTHIANS 6:19-20

I took the Word literally. My goal was to make it to Heaven. Psalm 119:11 says, *"Thy word have I hid in mine heart, that I might not sin against thee."* Therefore, it is important for children to learn the Word of God at an early age. No one can live or do what they do not know. The Word will protect us from mistakes, from sin, and keep us on the right path. I thank God for my childlike faith—I did not argue or analyze the Word. If God said it, I believed it, I lived it, and that settled it. Too many adults allow their minds, intellect, and worldviews to influence their belief in the Word of God. This causes stagnation in their spiritual growth, blindness in their spiritual eyes, and deafness in their spiritual ears. Jesus said in Luke 18:17, *"Verily I say unto you, whosoever shall not receive the kingdom of God as a little child shall in no wise enter therein."* And in Matthew 18:3, He said, *"Verily I say unto you, except ye be converted, and become as little children, ye shall not enter into the kingdom of heaven."*

My prayer is that I will never think that I have arrived, know it all, or have all wisdom and revelation but that I will remain like a child in my faith in God's Word. This has kept me humble before God, knowing that there is nothing He has called me to do that I can accomplish on my own. I need Him to empower me by the Holy Spirit to do the ministry He has entrusted me. As you read this book, may your faith become like that of a child, trusting God completely to do His work in your life and meet your needs. None of us is too far gone that God cannot reach us. If you have doubted His Word, repent and turn to the Lord. Ask Him for the grace to believe like a child and trust Him as a good Father.

Now join me as we enter 1978!

CHAPTER 3
TEENAGE YEARS AND 1978

If I had to pick the best year of my life, it would be 1978. Whenever I reflect on my life, I go back in memory to this time and season. It always brings me to tears when I remember the presence of God that I encountered in my home. I would pray, worship, sing, and cry out to God to use my life. There is a song I used to sing that was like a prayer to me. I am listing the entire song below because every verse and word spoke to me. I would cry out to the Lord to use my life, send me to the nations, and allow me to go for Him where no one wanted to go. I did not quite understand all that I was praying, but it came from my spirit. This was a precious season because God was very real to me. He captured my heart, and there was no turning back.

Jesus Use Me

Oh Lord, Please Don't Refuse Me,
For Surely There's A Work That I Can Do.
Even Though It's Humble,
Lord Help My Will To Crumble.

> Though The Cross Be Great, I'll Work For You.
> Dear Lord, I'll Be A Witness,
> If You Will Help My Weakness.
> I Know That I'm Not Worthy, Lord, Of You.
> By Eyes Of Faith, I See You, On The Cross Of Calvary.
> Dear Lord, I Cry, Let Me Thy Servant, Let Me Be.
> I'll Stand For Thee, Dear Jesus,
> 'Tho Death May Come My Way,
> I'll Spread The Gospel To The Fallen Here.
> But If It Be Thy Will, To Go Across The Sea,
> Lord, Help Me To Be Willing To Say Yes.
> He's The Lily Of The Valley,
> The Bright And Morning Star.
> He's The Fairest Of Ten Thousand To My Soul.
> He's The Beautiful Rose Of Sharon,
> He's All The World To Me.
> But Most Of All, He Is My Coming King.
> I'll Work For You, Dear Jesus,
> Wherever You May Send Me,
> Just Use Me So That Others May Be Blest.
> But If It Be Your Will, Lord,
> To Wait And Just Stand Still,
> Please Help Me To Be Willing To Say "Yes."

Growing up, I did not have many material things. But I was a teenager in love with Jesus and did not feel like I lacked anything. I never thought I was poor. He was enough! I did not have many friends, as most of my friends were not Christian. For those who were Christians, we did not share the same hunger for God. You will find many times in life that where God desires to take you, not many around you are going in the same direction, and to move forward, you will have to do so alone with God. I was in church, conventions, crusades, and church events, and I met many people but had few friends and acquaintances. For most of my journey, I walked alone with God. Unfortunately, many people we meet along life's way who are believers do not share our passion or hunger for the same things. Like Abraham and Lot, sometimes you will have to part ways with people so you can fulfill God's calling on your life.

Several significant events marked me in 1978 and made it the most memorable year of my life. The following four stand out:

WATER BAPTISM IN THE BIG CITY

One of the ordinances of the Bible is water baptism. I desired to be baptized as Jesus commanded:

> Go ye therefore, and teach all nations, baptizing them in the name of the Father, and of the Son, and of the Holy Ghost:
> Teaching them to observe all things whatsoever I have commanded you ...
>
> — MATTHEW 28:19-20

Since I did not have a church or pastor, we organized a trip to Central AOG Church in Georgetown for my baptism. My younger sister and I went. We were excited, as we rarely got to go on trips anywhere. It felt wonderful, like we were going on a field trip to meet the Lord Himself. The city was exciting, with paved streets, nice-looking buildings, and many large stores. It was our first time at the main church, and it was huge and beautiful, with a baptismal on the stage. When they asked us to share our testimony, we gladly took the mic (our first time speaking in a microphone) and boldly shared how the Lord had saved us and how we would serve Him forever. It was "country" coming to the "city," and we were happy to be there and share what God had done for us. After all the decades that have passed, we are still serving the Lord.

> Decree a thing, and it shall be established.
>
> —JOB 22:28

This event solidified my faith and put a stamp on me that I belonged to God and my life was no longer my own. I made up my mind to go all the way with Jesus, and no devil in Hell would stop me. That was the kind of determination I had then and still do now. Hallelujah!

BAPTISM IN THE HOLY GHOST AND SHOWDOWN BETWEEN BAPTIST AND PENTECOSTAL

When I first began to learn about the Holy Ghost Baptism, I wanted it. Actually, I wanted everything that God had for me. I heard my Sunday school teachers speaking in tongues and became hungry for this gift from the Lord. In those days, they would ask you, "Have you been filled?" or "When did you get filled?" I don't hear that nowadays. Among the young Pentecostals, it was about who spoke with tongues, who had the "Thompson Chain Reference Bible," or the latest gospel book they were reading that came from America. I wanted it all: the baptism of the Holy Ghost, the Thompson Chain Reference Bible, and the Christian gospel books. It is good to covet the good gifts.

> But covet earnestly the best gifts: and yet shew I unto you a more excellent way.
>
> — 1 CORINTHIANS 12:31

I devoured every book I received. Some were from Oral Roberts. I would write to ministries in America for books and other learning materials. I did many correspondence courses on various books of the Bible, like Acts and Romans, and would later receive my certificate in the mail. I was hungry and fed my soul. If you fill your heart, mind, and soul with God, His Word, good gospel books, songs, and hymns, it will strengthen you and help keep you from falling backward. You are not only what you eat but also what you read and hear.

> And it shall come to pass in the last days, saith God, I will pour out of my Spirit upon all flesh: and your sons and your daughters shall prophesy, and your young men shall see visions, and your old men shall dream dreams.
>
> — ACTS 2:17

I believed it.

Later that year, the church where I had been baptized in water invited me back to participate in a special service. Hundreds of young people were there, and the leaders encouraged us to seek the baptism in the Spirit. I began to pray and cry out to God to baptize me. I was desperate because I felt like I was missing out on this exciting spiritual experience that many already had. During this time, the Lord baptized me in the precious Holy Spirit with the evidence of speaking in tongues. I was ecstatic. I was part of the *Church Crowd* and felt like I was truly Pentecostal now.

> But ye shall receive power, after that the Holy Ghost is come upon you: and ye shall be witnesses unto me

> both in Jerusalem, and in all Judaea, and in Samaria, and unto the uttermost part of the earth.
>
> — ACTS 1:8

This is the power that helps us to be effective in our Christian life; it's the power to win souls for Christ and live a victorious life above reproach.

Now that I had received the Holy Ghost, it wasn't time to sit down but to go out and get busy for the Lord. I continued to serve in our Weekly Service to lead worship and teach Sunday school, but I continued to preach at the Ferry Terminal during the week. I would also look for opportunities to share the gospel one-on-one and pray for the sick. All I wanted was for God to use my life. To God be the glory for all He has done. I never wanted to be like other people and never wanted to be a lukewarm Christian. I always declared that my Christian life would not be ordinary. I have seen enough of that, and I wanted to be extraordinary. I desired to be all that God made me to be. We can settle for what we see in church and around us, or we can determine to believe what God said about us in His Word. I dare you to believe everything in the Bible, every chapter, every line, and every word. If God said it, I believe it, and that settles it. Amen!

This new power and fire of the Holy Ghost led to a showdown between the Baptist and Pentecostal believers. Remember in Luke 10:17, the disciples said, "Lord, even the devils are subject unto us through thy name." In our village, there was a young teenage girl who was demon-possessed. No one had ever seen a manifestation of demons before. I hadn't either, but I knew about it from reading the Bible. Jesus and His disciples cast out demons and set the captive free. The people in the home were terrified by what they saw and heard. The girl's mother-in-law took a broom and began beating her, trying to drive the demon out. When I saw this, I asked her to stop, explaining that she would hurt the girl.

> "And if Satan cast out Satan, he is divided against himself; how shall then his kingdom stand?"
>
> — MATTHEW 12:26

It takes the power of Christ to cast out demons, not human strength or methods.

In desperation, someone called the girl's Baptist pastor, who came and prayed fervently—but nothing happened. He clearly did not carry the power of the Holy Ghost, and the demon did not respond. He tried his best, but no deliverance came, and he eventually gave up. I had never been exposed to anything like this—we had no television to show how preachers handled demon-possessed people, no phones to call for help. My only reference was Jesus and the power of the Holy Ghost. Zachariah 4:6 reminds us, *"Not by might, nor by power, but by my Spirit, saith the Lord of hosts."*

Knowing what I knew from the Word and from what Jesus did, I stepped forward. It was showtime: Jesus is alive, He has conquered Hell and the grave, and this demon would bow to Him today. Everyone was afraid for me, worried that the demon might attack and hurt me, especially since earlier, the girl had taken a knife and tried to stab someone. She had strength and boldness that clearly didn't come from her alone. She probably weighed about 80 pounds, but I was unafraid because I felt the power of the Holy Ghost in me. So I spoke to the demon: "Come out of her in Jesus' name." I will never forget what happened next. The demon spoke to me through the girl in perfect English with a strong, male voice: "Jessica, what are you doing?"

Now, I need to explain something here. This girl did not speak proper English and had only completed elementary grades. Moreover, in my country, no one pronounced my name as "Jessica" in that way; they would usually say, "Jes-seeeeeee-ca," drawn out. This girl was clearly possessed by an older, English-speaking demon. Hearing the demon speak was startling, but it didn't intimidate me. I knew the Spirit of God within me was more powerful than any demon from Hell. She was delivered, and everyone, including our Baptist pastor friend, witnessed the power of Jesus Christ that day. This event marked me as a strong Pentecostal believer, transformed by the power of Christ that lives in me through the Holy Ghost.

Another significant showdown between the power of Christ and a stone god happened that same year. Growing up in South America, with warm weather year-round, most homes had ample yard space for vegetable and flower gardens. We had vegetables in the backyard and flowers in the front. My mom had reserved a part of the front yard to worship her god. One day, I was sweeping the yard, as we did every week. In this particular part of the flower garden was an oval stone, shaped like a large egg. My heart would ache to see my mom pour milk and place flowers on this stone as she prayed to it. Being a Christian on fire for God, I often did radical things, like handing out tracts at other religious events. Looking back, I'm thankful I didn't get shot or stoned!

While sweeping the flower garden one day, a holy indignation came over me, and I kicked the stone away. As I kicked it, I sang the song, "Roll this stone of hindrance away." Just then, my mom came out of the house and saw me. Now the showdown began. At the time, she wasn't a Christian and was furious at my disrespect. She said she would live to see the foot I used to kick the stone rot and fall off. My response was, "If this stone is greater than my God, we shall see." Well, she lived to be nearly ninety-six years old, and both my feet are still strong! I thank God she eventually came to know Jesus as her

Lord and Savior, placing her faith in a God who is alive, hears her prayers, and is not a stone. Praise the Lord! We must stand boldly and without shame for our faith.

> For I am not ashamed of the gospel of Christ: for it is the power of God unto salvation to every one that believeth; to the Jew first, and also to the Greek.
>
> — ROMANS 1:16

I am not ashamed of Jesus; in fact, I am proud to be a Christian.

MY GREATEST ACCOMPLISHMENT: READING THROUGH THE BIBLE FOR THE FIRST TIME IN 1978

> Thy word is a lamp unto my feet, and a light unto my path.
>
> — PSALMS 119:105

As my hunger for God grew, the Word became precious to me. I resolved to read through the entire Bible. I didn't personally know anyone in my community who had done this, though I'm sure there were many who loved God and His Word. I prayed for the Lord's grace to accomplish this goal despite schoolwork, homework, and mandatory chores. It's amazing what we can achieve when we set our minds to something. The Holy Spirit revealed many deep truths to me during this time, and the Word became not only precious but also real. No one who spends time reading and meditating on the Word of God will remain the same. Paul said,

> So then faith cometh by hearing, and hearing by the word of God.
>
> — ROMANS 10:17

My faith grew as I spent countless hours reading, and the Word took root in my heart, mind, and spirit. Faith doesn't only come from listening to preaching but also from reading the Bible; it is God speaking directly to us. You can never become a strong believer without spending time reading, studying, and meditating on the precious Word of God each day. He has given it to us for a purpose. It's His love letter to His bride. If you don't read it, you will never know what He has in store for you. I encourage everyone to read it like a storybook. Don't worry that you don't understand all of it. The Holy Spirit will reveal to you what you need now and will enable you to handle each stage of your journey. You cannot live what you don't know. Study the Word so you can take hold of all His promises for your life. Hear what Hosea 4:6 says, *"My people are destroyed* (or perish) *for lack of knowledge."* Many of God's children suffer because they don't know His Word. It is our spiritual food; without it, we will suffer spiritual starvation.

Read the Word and take hold of all the promises God has for you. Read the Word and it will make you strong and give you a firm foundation for the rest of your life. For young people, if you will read and believe the Word of God, it will keep you pure, protect you, and lead you in a straight path. It will prevent you from many of the pitfalls the devil set to trap you and derail your destiny. Everything on earth will pass away one day, but we can rely on God's Word to stand forever.

> Heaven and earth shall pass away: but my words shall not pass away.
>
> — MARK 13:31

It makes sense to build our lives on such a firm, eternal foundation. Amen!

FIRST FAST: 14 DAYS IN 1978

> Moreover when ye fast, be not, as the hypocrites, of a sad countenance… but thou, when thou fastest, anoint thine head, and wash thy face; That thou appear not unto men to fast, but unto thy Father which is in secret: and thy Father, which seeth in secret, shall reward thee openly.
>
> — MATTHEW 6:16-18

The Holy Spirit prompted me to fast, and my desire to know God was so intense that nothing else mattered. When we fast, we must have a purpose, or else the enemy will tempt us. If the purpose is not clearly defined and the end result not important enough, it will be easy to fall and quit. Once, while fasting for my parents, I was tempted by a Doritos chip. Hungry as I was, I remembered why I was fasting, and that one chip was not worth giving up on seeing the results I was believing God for. Be wary of the temptation to quit or to give in to the passion for food when you decide to fast. Keep the purpose in the forefront of your mind. It will help you to persevere to completion. For the first three days, the hunger pangs felt unbearable, but my desire for God was greater than my physical hunger so I persevered and won the battle against my flesh. Day after day, I read the Word, prayed, and worshiped the Lord as I continued my journey of fasting. I still had to go to school, do homework, do chores at home, and teach Sunday School. Except for losing some weight (I did not have much to start with), I gained physical and spiritual strength. Fasting is not about merely abstaining from food; it's about prayer, seeking God, reading His Word, and being in His presence. If we don't pray when fasting, it's merely a diet.

In his book *Fasting – Atomic Power with God*, Franklin Hall says, "A twenty-one or forty-day prayer and fast will most assuredly hasten the Christian to such a deep and wonderful experience with God that twenty-one days will equal twenty-one years. Forty days will equal forty years. Experience shows that forty-day period brings far greater results than a shorter time. It will bring one closer to God more quickly than any other way known." He goes on to say, "Fasting is the most potent power of the universe and is placed at the disposal of every believer." I encourage every believer to endeavor to do a twenty-one or forty-day fast. This is only if you are desperate to see restoration and acceleration in your life. I have done one forty-day fast and results were unbelievable, the answers were quick, the revelation was life-changing, and the doors opened supernaturally. Maybe you have wasted some years and wish they can be restored to you because you want to accomplish some things for the Lord. It's not too late. If you are willing, God will give you the grace. The secret is how hungry are you for Him, how thirsty are you to know Him more, and how desperate are you for God to use your life. God says in Joel 2:25 *"And I will restore to you the years that the locust hath eaten, the cankerworm, and the caterpiller, and the palmerworm, my great army which I sent among you."* The Psalmist David was a man after God's heart, he penned in Psalms 42:1-2 his thirst for God *"As the deer panteth after the water brooks, so panteth my soul after thee, O God. My soul thirsteth for God, for the living God: when shall I come and appear before God?"* Do you desire God like this? If you do, it will lead you to action and action precedes the blessings. Make up your mind today that you will go after God in Prayer and Fasting. You will not regret it but will testify someday of the blessing of this experience. You will not be the same.

This experience impacted my life as a young girl and led me to pursue more and more of His presence. It led me on a spiritual path that I could never have fathomed. My life was never the same. It set me apart from my peers in and out of the Church circle. Deep within my heart, something different happened to me. I felt the calling of God on my life more clearly and I knew without a shadow of a doubt that I would serve Him till the day I die. He has made Himself real to me.

> And I will restore to you the years that the locust hath eaten…
>
> —JOEL 2:25

Like the psalmist, my soul pants for God, longing to know Him more. This experience in 1978 set me on a path I could never have imagined, making that year one of my most cherished.

Join me as the journey continues across the great Atlantic, from South America to North America.

CHAPTER 4
CROSSING THE ATLANTIC—WELCOME TO AMERICA THE BEAUTIFUL

The dawning of a new decade—the 1980s—found me on a new continent, in a country that seemed like a fairy tale. I remember touching down at JFK International Airport in New York at night and seeing a sea of lights everywhere. My teenage mind could barely take it all in. It was true what they said: America was the land of the free, the home of the brave, and a land where money grew on trees. At least, that's how people saw America back then. The beauty of the city mesmerized me. I had never seen anything like it before. Could this be what Heaven would be like? The view from above the city was amazing—a spectacular sight. I wondered if we could view life from above, from God's perspective, how differently we would live.

> These things I have spoken unto you, that in me ye might have peace. In the world ye shall have tribulation: but be of good cheer; I have overcome the world.
>
> —JOHN 16:33

Because He overcame, we shall as well.

It did not take long before I became homesick. I missed my friends, my life, and my church. Even though life had been hard and I didn't have much, I still wanted to return to the life I knew and the familiarity of it. Like the Children of Israel when they came out of Egypt, they murmured and complained to Moses, wanting to go back to the land that had them in bondage. They missed the garlic and leeks:

> We remember the fish, which we did eat in Egypt freely; the cucumbers, and the melons, and the leeks, and the onions, and the garlick.
>
> — NUMBERS 11:5

They forgot how much their taskmasters whipped them to make stone from straw. They could not see a promised land flowing with milk and honey waiting for them, and God was taking them there as He had promised. My family was here. Our home, land, and everything else we owned were gone—sold. There was nothing to go back to. It took a few years to settle down and accept that I wasn't going back, and this was my new home. God has a plan for you and me, and it is big! Say, "I believe it!"

Change is not always easy, but it is necessary at times. There were prayers I prayed that God would answer here. I realized that God always hears and answers our prayers. It may not always be when we want, but He is never late.

> Call unto me, and I will answer thee, and show thee great and mighty things, which thou knowest not.
>
> — JEREMIAH 33:3

I came with a list of four things that I was believing God for: a guitar, a Thompson Chain Reference Bible, a camera, and a tape recorder. It seems like a strange combination, but it was my heart's desire, and the Lord gave me all four. My Thompson Chain Reference Bible from 1982, which I still have, is my most prized and cherished possession. It cost $40, which was one-third of my weekly salary then.

The first time I saw snow was mind-blowing. There is absolutely nothing as white as snow. One morning, I was walking to a job I had about 15 minutes away from home. It was early, and I was the only one walking then. The snow was about 10 inches deep. As I walked, I looked in front of me at the smooth, white snow everywhere. I could not see the sidewalk, the road, or any dirt. Everything was totally covered and looked white and clean. It was beautiful to my eyes and marvelous to behold. It was so white that my eyes dazzled from its glare. Then I remembered the Bible verse:

> Come now, and let us reason together, saith the Lord: though your sins be as scarlet, they shall be as white as snow; though they be red like crimson, they shall be as wool.
>
> — ISAIAH 1:18

I looked at the snow and realized there is nothing that can take away the stain of sin in our hearts but the blood of Jesus and make us as clean and white as snow. As I stood and stared at the snow, I concluded that nothing I had ever seen was as white as the whiteness of snow. Now I know what the Lord means when I read the verse. I was so touched looking at the snow and so moved by the revelation that tears came to my eyes as I continued to walk. I felt such joy in my heart that I didn't feel the cold of winter. Instead, I began to sing along the way: "Oh precious is the flow, that makes me white as snow, no other fount I know, nothing but the blood of Jesus."

That day, I felt that America was a beautiful place, and I thanked God for giving me this opportunity to live here and be part of this great country. I am forever grateful for the freedom we have in this country and thankful for those who gave their lives to purchase and retain that freedom. May we glorify God in America, and may a great awakening sweep this land from sea to shining sea. Whatever God is doing and will do in this nation, I want to be right smack in the center of it. Use me, Lord!

CHAPTER 5
THE EARLY DAYS OF MINISTRY IN NEW YORK

It was spring in New York, but coming from a tropical climate, it felt cold to me. My first thought was to find a church. The Lord led me to a Full Gospel, Pentecostal, Bible-believing church with a wonderful pastor and a growing congregation. Since I was used to working in the church and serving the Lord, I could not wait to get started in Sunday school and Children's Ministry. After about one month of attending church at Community Gospel in Queens, NY, I began assisting in Sunday school with the kindergarten kids. I did not believe in just coming to church; I believed in getting involved in ministry. It is always an honor to serve the Lord.

> Do not despise these small beginnings.
>
> — ZECHARIAH 4:10 (NLT)

Everywhere we would move, I would find a church and get involved. There is always a need for workers in children's ministry. I was happy and enjoyed where the Lord had me.

However, this would be my home church for only one and a half years, as my dad moved our family south to the forgotten borough of New York City called Staten Island, known as the "Borough of Parks." My father was always a pioneer, breaking away from the crowd and moving far away. In Guyana, he moved the family to the Northwest District and lived in Mabaruma. The only means of transportation was by boat—kids traveled by boat to school, and people rarely traveled there from the city or inland. It was a long, hard, and treacherous journey. This is where I was born. Mostly natives, called Amerindians, lived in this area. About twenty years after my family moved back inland, this area became known worldwide when the Jim Jones tragedy occurred in this region in 1978. When we moved to Staten Island, the population was four hundred thousand, which was very small compared to a city of eight million. There were only two ways to get there from the other boroughs—the Verrazano-Narrows Bridge or the Staten Island Ferry. It seemed water always surrounded the places my dad would move to, and you needed a boat or ferry to get in and out. People did not have easy access to these places. To keep people out of Staten Island, they would raise the bridge toll so high to prevent too many from coming or moving in. I never thought to ask him why, and I wish he were here now so I could find out this mystery. This island would become home for us and hold a lot of memories from our younger days in high school and college until my parents left Staten Island for their final, eternal, and heavenly home.

In Staten Island, I served at three different churches in Sunday school and Children's Ministry. The first was Stapleton Community Church, with Pastor Frank Crosby at a storefront church. Then it was Faith Christian Center with Pastor George Samuels at a strip mall church. Later, I served at ICC, or International Christian Center, with Pastor Hodgins. I enjoyed serving the Lord and count it a privilege that God would include me in what He is doing.

> And I thank Christ Jesus our Lord, who hath enabled me, for that he counted me faithful, putting me into the ministry.
>
> — 1 TIMOTHY 1:12

This verse of Scripture means a ton to me. I never felt worthy of the great opportunities the Lord had given me. Compared to my contemporaries, I didn't think I had what it takes, but God sees what man cannot see. He saw my heart.

> For the Lord seeth not as man seeth; for man looketh on the outward appearance, but the Lord looketh on the heart.
>
> — 1 SAMUEL 16:7

In the early 90s, I would travel back to Queens to attend another church and serve in ministry at Calvary Assembly. This time, I would not only teach Sunday school and Children's Church but also work with Youth Ministry as CA Secretary and occasionally speak at the youth service. CA, or Christ Ambassador, was the Youth Ministry of the Assemblies of God. Wherever the Lord planted me, I would give my best and honor Him with my commitment.

> Whatsoever thy hand findeth to do, do it with thy might …
>
> — ECCLESIASTES 9:10

Anything we do for the Lord should be done with joy, with all our might, and with our whole heart. God deserves our best because He gave us His best—His only begotten Son, Jesus Christ, who died on a cruel cross to save us from Hell. This alone is enough reason for me to serve Him all the days of my life. Hallelujah!

CHAPTER 6
I SHALL NOT DIE BEFORE MY TIME

God promised me: *"With long life I will satisfy you and show you my salvation"* (Psalm 91:16).

God's Word promises to protect and keep us. None of us shall die before our time. If you are reading this, then you are alive and have much to be thankful for. From our birth to now, the enemy has tried to take many of us out by various means, but God has kept us for His plans and purposes here on earth. I loved swimming as a child, and I came close to drowning on more than one occasion. When I was about eleven years old, I clearly remember doing a high dive from a bridge, and I went so deep that I hit my head on a tree trunk at the bottom of the canal. I saw sparkles and stars, but the Lord kept me, and I was able to come up to the surface. If I had lost consciousness, I would have drowned. Declare the Bible verse below over your life and the lives of your loved ones.

> I shall not die, but live, and declare the works of the Lord.
>
> — PSALM 118:17

There were three major events in my life where the Devil tried to take me out, but God had a plan for my life and brought me through. I have declared that I will not die before my time but will live to declare the Word of the Lord in my generation. If we could see a video of our life from when we were born to now, showing how many times God protected us, it would blow our minds. Maybe we will see such a video in Heaven. I can't wait to see it, for I know of many, many times that He has protected me.

> The thief cometh not, but for to steal, and to kill, and to destroy: I am come that they might have life, and that they might have it more abundantly.
>
> —JOHN 10:10

There is an enemy who wants us dead, preventing us from fulfilling the plans that God has for us. Especially if we are people of prayer, the Devil will try to get us out of that place because he knows the power of prayer.

In July 1996, I was traveling to Paris and was supposed to be on TWA Flight 800 out of JFK. But somehow, instead of leaving on Wednesday, I left on Tuesday. One hour after takeoff, we returned to JFK due to navigation problems. They fixed the issue, and we later took off to my destination. While in Paris, I saw the only English-speaking news channel broadcasting about a TWA Flight 800 that crashed in New York. I thought this was some documentary, as I had just come in the day before on this flight to Paris. Family members began to call frantically, as they thought I was on this flight. Just minutes after takeoff, all 250 passengers and crew on board perished when this flight crashed in New York. I was almost afraid to come back home on a TWA flight in light of what had happened. When I returned home, I discovered something very interesting on my wall calendar. I had checked off two possible days to travel: Tuesday, 7/16/96, or Thursday, 7/18/96. The flight crashed on Wednesday, 7/17/96. I shudder to think what would have happened if I had decided to travel on that day. I saw the hand of God protecting and guiding me. He must have a plan for my life, and I don't want to miss it. I am happy to be alive. God has been good to me.

> With long life will I satisfy him, and shew him my salvation.
>
> — PSALM 91:16

> He guards the paths of the just
> and protects those who are faithful to him.
>
> — PROVERBS 2:8 (NLT)

I am sure many can testify how God has protected them from imminent death. He is a good and faithful God.

The Psalmist declared:

> The LORD is my shepherd; I shall not want.
> He maketh me to lie down in green pastures: he leadeth me beside the still waters.
> He restoreth my soul: he leadeth me in the paths of righteousness for his name's sake.
> Yea, though I walk through the valley of the shadow of death, I will fear no evil: for thou art with me; thy rod and thy staff they comfort me.
> Thou preparest a table before me in the presence of mine enemies: thou anointest my head with oil; my cup runneth over.

JESSICA SEETARAM

> Surely goodness and mercy shall follow me all the days of my life: and I will dwell in the house of the Lord for ever.
>
> — PSALM 23:1-6

I believe God's Word and no devil in hell will stop my life short.

September 11, 2001, was surreal. It was a beautiful Tuesday morning. The temperature was 73 degrees, a perfect day. The sky was blue, and the sun was bright. I traveled from the Staten Island Ferry to the first train that would take me to the World Trade Center. My office was at 3 World Financial Center, and I would cross over the overpass to get to our building. It was early, around 8:40 a.m., and I decided to go to Duane Reade Drug Store in the WTC to buy snacks for the office. As I stood in line for the cashier, I heard the Spirit say not to buy snacks today but to go directly to the office. I put the snacks back and exited the WTC building for my office. While in the elevator, I saw on the TV screen a fire at the WTC. I didn't think much of it. When I got to our floor, no one was there. This surprised me, as there were always people there before 9 a.m. One colleague came in, and we began to wonder where everyone was. We decided to go to the windows facing the WTC, and there we saw a huge fire high up in the building. Someone said it was a helicopter that hit the building. My thoughts were that the firemen would put out the fire. I never thought anyone would die.

My colleague and I decided to go to another part of our building to get a better view of what was happening. As we stared across the street at the WTC, we saw a plane crash into the building. I knew then it was a terrorist attack. We grabbed our things and headed out of the building. By now, they had announced that everyone should evacuate. Panic and fear set in as people began to run out of the building, using the stairs. My friend and I ran out to Church Street and stood looking up at the WTC and the huge gaping hole. We stood in shock as we saw people from about eighty stories high jumping for their lives. They either stayed and burned alive or jumped. I remember praying, "Lord, who will catch them?" Many jumped to their deaths. My friend decided to head home to the NJ Ferry, and I decided to head to the Staten Island Ferry. We never thought the buildings would implode. That thought never crossed our minds.

As I walked away from the WTC, suddenly, people began to run. I was in the crowd and started running too, but I didn't know why. People were running into stores and restaurants—anywhere they could find shelter. I ran into a bodega to hide. After about five minutes, everyone came out. When I asked what was happening, people said there was a bomb, but no one was sure anymore. I headed toward Wall Street and kept running. After a few minutes, I stopped to look back and saw the WTC building engulfed in flames. I thought I had better get out of there because the top part of the building might fall, and debris would fly everywhere. I began to run, but my legs felt heavy, like in a bad dream. There was confusion and panic. White smoke poured out of the Whitehall Street subway station. Some people said it was a bomb in the subway. I felt like this was it—I was going to die. I asked the Lord that if I was going to die, let it be quick so I do not suffer. I made it to the last ferry out of Manhattan. After that, they converted the ferry into a morgue for the WTC victims. Everyone grabbed life jackets, thinking they would bomb the ferry next. People began to pray loudly and cry out unashamedly to God for His protection. As the ferry left Manhattan and was halfway across the East River to Staten Island, I looked back, and all I could see was white smoke. Nothing was visible as smoke covered Lower Manhattan. At this point, I didn't know that both towers had imploded. The New York City skyline would never be the same.

If the Lord had not warned me about not buying the snacks, or if I had not heeded His voice, I would have died that day or suffered serious injuries. The time it would have taken me to wait in line, pay for my snacks, and walk outside would have been the exact moment and place where the first plane hit and debris fell. This would have been the spot where I would have been walking, and if I had been there, I would have been hit by the debris. When the first plane hit, I was in our elevator going up to my office. I am so thankful for the Holy Spirit and for the ability to hear and obey Him. I am still here, and I will fulfill God's plan for my life in my lifetime. The Devil has lost again. America went to church on Sunday following the 9/11 attack on the WTC, but it wasn't long before people forgot God and went back to their old ways of living.

> Be sober, be vigilant; because your adversary the devil, as a roaring lion, walketh about, seeking whom he may devour.
>
> — 1 PETER 5:8

Listen and obey the voice of the Spirit quickly when He speaks. You never know what He is saving you from. Amen.

Another close call came in 2011 on I-95 in the state of Georgia. I was driving from New York to Florida. It was a beautiful, sunny day, and I was worshipping the Lord in song and praise when suddenly, a Jeep pulling a trailer struck me in the left lane. The impact sliced through my passenger side door from front to back and sent my vehicle spinning out of control. Immediately, I began to plead the blood of Jesus. In that moment, I experienced the protective power of His blood. I didn't pray any other prayer—just kept pleading the blood of Jesus.

As my vehicle continued to spin out of control in the left lane, it started drifting toward a ravine. Just then, it felt as if the Lord sent the biggest and strongest angel to stop the vehicle from toppling over. The front wheels got stuck in the mud, and the vehicle came to a halt. The driver who hit me pulled over, convinced that whoever was inside would not have survived. He called 911, and when the paramedics arrived and took our vitals, they found that none of us had elevated blood pressure or pulse. While the vehicle was spinning, it felt as if the Lord had suspended us in midair. There were no bruises or injuries.

We prayed with the paramedics and even led them to the Lord. They were shocked that we survived. The Lord's hand was on my life and those with me in the vehicle. I never want to forget the goodness of the Lord and His divine protection.

> The angel of the Lord encampeth round about them that fear him, and delivereth them."
>
> — PSALMS 34:7

We are all here for a purpose. Seek what God has planned for you and pursue it wholeheartedly so that your life on earth will have meaning—and in Heaven, you will gain many stars in your crown.

CHAPTER 7
A PLACE OF SPIRITUAL DISCONTENT

As stated before, everywhere I lived, I would find a church and serve. I could never be comfortable just sitting and receiving in church; I had to be active and do something for the Lord. As the late 90s rolled around, I began to feel spiritually jittery. I started feeling uncomfortable and didn't really understand why. Church did not seem to satisfy whatever was in my heart—the longing, the emptiness, and the lack of knowing. I am sure many people felt this but did not know why or what to do. I did not attend the prayer meetings because they seemed dead and boring. Besides, it seemed like only old ladies and old men were the ones mostly there. Something was brewing in my heart that I couldn't identify. There was no one to talk to about it. What I saw were lots of "religious" people who loved God but settled for doing what they knew, what they had seen, and what they had learned. I didn't see a hunger for God or His presence. Everyone seemed comfortable, and there was no need to press in further for more.

> O God, thou art my God; early will I seek thee: my
> soul thirsteth for thee, my flesh longeth for thee in
> a dry and thirsty land, where no water is.
>
> — PSALM 63:1

This is how I felt. A hunger and thirst for God and a move of the Spirit were beginning to well up in me. I felt desperate for something more. I have always said that I would not be an ordinary Christian. I did not want to settle for church as usual or just go through the motions. I believe God is infinite and desires to do great and mighty things in and through every believer's life. But too quickly, we settle for the ordinary and mundane when God has promised us so much more.

> The thief cometh not, but for to steal, and to kill, and
> to destroy: I am come that they might have life,
> and that they might have it more abundantly.
>
> — JOHN 10:10

I wanted this life, even though I didn't understand what it entailed. I hadn't heard in church how I could aspire to great things in God or be all that God created me to be. So, I began to pray. What a novel idea!

While I continued to serve where I was, my heart was changing. I desired more meat of the Word; I wanted to see God move in His church like we read in the Book of Acts. But it wasn't happening. The more I prayed and sought God, the more my heart began to change. I realized that either I had to change or the place needed to change. May I say that change is good sometimes? Some people stay in the same place all their lives and never desire more. But if you want to see God use your life in a greater way, you will be more than willing to change as He leads you.

> But we all, with open face beholding as in a glass the glory of the Lord, are changed into the same image from glory to glory, even as by the Spirit of the Lord.
>
> — 2 CORINTHIANS 3:18

It was never meant for us to stay in the same spiritual or physical condition all the days of our lives, but to grow, expand, increase, move up, and move on from glory to glory. The moment a believer begins to pray, things will start to change. It first starts in our minds, then in our hearts, and after that, our actions will follow suit.

> Let this mind be in you, which was also in Christ Jesus.
>
> — PHILIPPIANS 2:5

Spiritual discontent—or spiritual hunger and thirst—is the most powerful motivator in the Christian life. No one will stay still or remain the same when experiencing this desire for God. It will lead to changes in your prayer life, your time in the Word of God, fasting, reading books on revival, seeking out great revival meetings, and anointed preaching. It may sometimes even lead to physical relocation. Your priorities will begin to change, how you spend your time and your day will change, and your goals and desires will change. Nothing will stand in your way. As you pursue God, He will lead you, open doors, and provide supernaturally. The four lepers in 2 Kings 7:3 realized this and said, *"Why sit we here until we die?"* They recognized that they were outcasts and would die anyway, so they decided to rise up and take their chances. They took action, got up, moved forward, and lived.

Do not stay in a dead church and miss your purpose in life. No one will care about your spiritual condition more than you. Our allegiance is not to man but to God, so do not be afraid to make a move if God is speaking to you and leading you. We do not dishonor spiritual authority or leadership over our lives, but we do not make gods out of our pastors and leaders or become dependent on people to supply all our spiritual needs. Do not be lazy to pray or read and study the Word. Especially if you know that God has called you and has a great plan for your life, you must move toward it, or you will die without fulfilling your destiny. Do not take what God has given you to the grave—let the world see it, know it, and be blessed by it. You are salt, and the world needs your flavor. You were born with a purpose to fulfill the Great Commission. Don't miss out!

As the year 2000 rolled around, the Lord directed me to move to another church on Staten Island. I didn't know it then, but it would be my last tour of duty on the island where my parents lived and raised us. Once again, I served in the Children's Ministry faithfully. This was all I knew, and it was all I did. I was good at it because I had been doing it for twenty-four years by that time. I didn't need much prayer or study for the lessons. Honestly, I could wing it, and I did many times. There was no dependence on the Holy Ghost or the anointing. It became routine and ritualistic. But a few months later, everything in my life was about to undergo a radical transformation. Come with me as we journey into Y2K and the greatest encounter of my life. Nothing—and I mean nothing—will ever be the same.

CHAPTER 8
Y2K—MY GREATEST VICTORY WON – DESPERATION LEADS TO TRANSFORMATION

The world was on edge as we entered the new year and decade. Widespread concern arose about a computer programming shortcut that was expected to cause extensive havoc as the year changed from 1999 to 2000. Corporations spent millions of dollars to test their systems, ensuring that business would run smoothly as they crossed over into a new millennium. The scare was apocalyptic, but the world entered the new year without incident. The programmers had done their jobs well, and everyone could breathe a sigh of relief.

While the world was caught up in Y2K, I found myself caught up in a spiritual wilderness and desperate for an escape route. Life didn't seem to have meaning, and material things did not satisfy. I felt like running away from everything but didn't know where to go. I felt like the psalmist:

> As the hart panteth after the water brooks, so panteth my soul after thee ...
>
> — PSALM 42:1

> My tears have been my meat day and night ...
>
> — PSALM 42:3

How many of you can identify?

> Why art thou cast down, O my soul? ...
>
> — PSALM 42:5

Yes, I felt like there was no hope, so how could I even praise God? Verse 7 says, *"Deep calleth unto deep."* Something deep in my soul was crying out, but I didn't know for what. It seemed like there was a hole in my heart that nothing in this world could fill. Mind you, I had been saved, filled with the Holy Ghost, and serving in ministry. You might ask why Christians go through certain wilderness experiences. Remember, the apostle Paul was in Arabia for three years, and Jesus was in the wilderness for forty days. In these seasons, we walk alone with God. No outside influence exists. During these times, if we press into God, we will emerge stronger, closer to God, and built up in faith to face anything that comes our way.

As you read this, I want you to know that God is faithful to His Word. You can trust Him when nothing makes sense in your life or circumstances. *They that hunger and thirst after righteousness shall be filled* (Matthew 5:6). It was now June 2000, and the world had quieted down around January 1, 2000. It was now in the past, but I was facing my future as my journey continued.

It was Friday evening, June 4, 2000, when I came home from work. I felt restless, like something was about to happen. I wasn't sure what to do. Again, I felt like running to a place called "nowhere," but instead, I grabbed my favorite Bible and went to my kitchen table downstairs. This was about 10 p.m. At the kitchen table, I began to weep and worship the Lord. After a while, I started to pray. As the night progressed, I found myself engulfed in God's presence. With snot running out of my nose, mingled with tears pouring from my eyes, I worshipped.

For two hours, I prayed, cried, worshipped, and sang until my body shook. Suddenly, there came travailing prayers from deep in my belly like I had never experienced before. The presence and glory of God filled the space where I was sitting, and for the first time in my life, I felt like I had touched Heaven in my prayer. I remember opening my Bible and singing a song verbatim that, to this day, I cannot locate. I have combed through the Bible cover to cover, from Genesis to Revelation, over five times, looking for the song, but I could not find it. I'm not sure if it came right out of my spirit. But the words were: *"I will praise thee, Lord, with every breath that I take. I will praise thee, Lord; this promise I make. And should eternity end and start all over again, even then I will praise thee, Lord."* I sang this song over and over until it became an anthem to me. Revival had stirred in my soul, and everything, including my ministry, was about to change. My life would never be the same again.

During this two-hour prayer session, I asked the Lord for one thing and made a promise to Him. Three years prior, I had trouble sleeping at night, so I asked the Lord if He gave me good sleep and allowed me to rest at night, I would serve Him all the days of my life. I don't mean winging it, but from the depths of my heart and soul, I would serve Him with all of me. I would step out and do what He asked, even if I felt unqualified. I would trust Him completely. I would trust His will for my life, His call, and His plans for me. I would give it all to Him and never look back. From that night on, I have slept like a baby. No matter what storms have come my way, the Lord has granted me good sleep, and no devil can take it away. He answered that prayer, and I kept my promise. But there is more!

This encounter with the Lord on that Friday night changed me completely. When I rose from my kitchen table, I became a different person, and I felt like a huge weight had been lifted off my back. All of a sudden, life came back to me, hope returned, purpose returned, and the future looked bright and promising once again. I felt the birth of prayer in my heart, soul, and spirit that night. I had never heard of deep travailing or deep intercessory prayer before. What the Lord deposited in me that night does not compare to anything I had experienced in church or in my walk with God before. Prayer does change everything—it's not just a cliché but a fact. Anyone who prays consistently and fervently will never remain the same. I seemed to be walking on cloud nine. The surrounding people may not have known what was going on, but I was on a mission and a new journey with God.

> Behold, I will do a new thing; now it shall spring forth; shall ye not know it? I will even make a way in the wilderness, and rivers in the desert.
>
> — ISAIAH 43:19

I was jumping, leaping, and praising God.

The next day was Saturday, a day when shopping, cleaning, cooking, and laundry were done. I woke up with much strength and finished all the chores by early afternoon because I couldn't wait to lock myself away and pray. I felt like He was pursuing me to lock myself away with Him. It felt like my "first love" had been restored.

> My beloved spake, and said unto me, Rise up, my love, my fair one, and come away.
>
> — SONG OF SOLOMON 2:10

He was calling me unto Himself. My heart was panting for His presence. Every day, I couldn't wait to get alone with God in prayer, not just once but as many times as possible. I had touched something of His presence that was so sweet, and I couldn't get enough.

No ministry or person can do anything great for God without a strong and consistent prayer life. We should do everything for God on the foundation of prayer because "Not by might, nor by power, but by my spirit, saith the Lord of hosts" (Zechariah 4:6). I have come to understand something: Christians who do not pray consistently and fervently are missing out on all that God has for them. So many people who love the Lord are living below the level that God desires or has planned for them. What would happen if every Christian began to do what Jeremiah 33:3 says: *"Call unto me, and I will answer thee, and show thee great and mighty things, which thou knowest not"*? Or as James 4:2 says, *"You have not because you ask not."* None of us know all that God has in store for us, and it's not until we desperately cry out to Him that things will begin to change. Many believers only ask God for what they can do or accomplish themselves, so no faith is required.

The greatest aspect of our Christian life is our prayer life. This is what changes us. It's what draws God closer to us and into our situation. It's what includes and involves God in our daily life. Once God becomes part of our daily life through prayer, nothing will remain the same. Trust me on this!

Many people love God and love to be in His house, but sometimes hate going to church. This isn't because they don't want to be there but because they feel bored; nothing in the church is motivating or encouraging. Hear me—I felt that way until I had my encounter with the Lord. Afterward, I became the thermostat; I set the temperature. I went to the same church, happy, joyful, and excited to worship. Nothing in the church or around me changed, but my heart had changed. I no longer went hoping that a song or message would uplift me. Instead, I went with the attitude that I would worship the Lord.

I would bring something to church and receive whatever the Lord had for me. If I got something, that was great, but if not, I would bring my worship, my prayers, my praise, my adoration, my tithes and offerings, and give them to the Lord. My whole outlook and perspective changed, although things in the church remained the same. Prayer will change your heart, your thinking, and how you see the world, how you view God, the church, and people. In the presence of God, we become like Him—our hearts begin to love the things He loves and hate the things He hates. From the inside out, we are changing. I pray that none of you who read this book will remain the same but that a fire will begin to burn in your belly for the very tangible presence of God, and your hunger and thirst will propel you to go deep—very deep. Amen!

When you are seeking God, you will find that the more you experience Him and His glorious presence, the more you learn and the more you get to know Him, the less you seem to know and the more you want. He is infinite. As your hunger deepens, your thirst becomes more desperate, and you keep pressing in more intensely. It's amazing that once you have tasted and seen that the Lord is good, you cannot go back to living life as you did before. Neither can you tolerate sin, whether in or out of the church. You become very sensitive to the Holy Spirit and much more discerning. You find there is more clarity, revelation, and spiritual eyesight. Things you didn't see and hear before, even though they were right in front of you, are clear now. Your spiritual antennas are up—not to criticize or condemn but to confirm the Word. Deception won't easily trick you. Amen!

You can spot a fake preacher a mile away and know when a preacher is teaching false doctrines. You will experience boldness in your faith to share the gospel and stand up for truth like never before. Your faith will grow stronger to believe God for impossible things in your life. You will make up your mind to run hard after God and never go back to the old life. This new life is too good, too sweet, and too precious to trade for anything this world has to offer. It's you and God, and together, you will be more than conquerors. While life around you may not change much and circumstances may remain the same, somehow, none of these will faze you. You move forward to a different sound and hear His whisperings: "Walk here," "Don't go there." You finally hear and understand His voice. Oh, how long you wished you could hear His voice, but you were never close enough to Him to hear it. Now that you are praying so often, your ears are attentive to the Spirit's promptings daily. Wow! You realize you've come a long way, baby, and God has got you. His perfect love casts out every fear in your heart about the future. Amen!

As your hunger and thirst for Him grow deeper and stronger, prayer alone is not enough. The desire to get into the Word also becomes greater. I started reading from Genesis to Revelation over and over. Many times, the Holy Spirit would reveal deep truths to me. He became my greatest teacher. I'm not saying we don't need the fivefold ministry. But when we spend time in the Word, the Holy Spirit will speak to us. This later led to a deeper study of the Word. The more I read, the sweeter the Word of God became to me. I couldn't get enough. I planned my day around my prayer time and time in the Word. God had captured my heart, and all of me belonged to Him.

The next thing the Holy Spirit impressed upon my heart was to fast. Nothing will accelerate your walk with God, increase the anointing, give clear direction, or open doors more than fasting. Growing up in church, I didn't see much fasting or hear people or pastors talk about it. Many around me seemed satisfied with the status quo and didn't prioritize fasting. Don't get me wrong. I'm sure many fasted, but I didn't see or hear about it. Hunger for God, for His will to be accomplished in your life, will push you to go further step by step. In 2 Corinthians 3:18, the Bible says, *"But we all, with open face beholding as in a glass the glory of the Lord, are changed into the same image from glory to glory, even as by the Spirit of the Lord."* God desires for us to keep moving forward—higher, deeper with Him—from glory to glory, and not remain stale and stagnant.

As stated before, apart from my salvation, this revival at my kitchen table has been the greatest experience of my life. It changed my life and direction forever. For the first time, I could hear the voice of God. People ask all the time, "How do you hear the voice of God?" Well, you have to know Him, and you get to know Him when you spend time with Him in prayer and in the Word. As you become familiar with the way God speaks to you, you will have clear direction as to what to do, where to go, where to live, where to serve, and the ministry He calls you to. He speaks to each of us differently—the way He knows us and how we will respond. He may not speak to you the same way He speaks to me. He knows each of us individually and deals with us on that basis.

Another thing that became so clear and evident from this experience was the revelation of the Word. Many times, while studying the Word, the Holy Spirit would take a verse I had known since Sunday school days and explode a revelation that would change me. This happened repeatedly. He became my greatest teacher. The more I received, the hungrier I got. The Word of God became so precious to me. It was precious before, but this was different. It was sweet. I cherished the time I spent reading and studying and how God spoke to me through His Word. All of this helped build a solid foundation for what was to come.

Never had I gotten answers to prayer so quickly. I remember that in the past, I would pray and pray for things, and it would take forever for the answer to come. Now, the answers seemed to come so quickly.

Often, He would answer a desire of my heart without me even praying for it. It blew me away. This is when I realized how much God loves me. Only when you come to the place where you not only realize but also know the height and depth of God's love for you will it change you completely. You will never crave or depend on human love to affirm you when you know the true love of God. Wow! I hope you grasp this. You may have been saved a long time, but you have not yet experienced His love. You know in your heart He loves you, but you can't feel it. Ask the Lord to reveal His love to you in tangible ways, and He will do it. Remember James 4:2: *"You have not because you ask not."* Step out and ask God for big things. Don't be afraid or ashamed.

> Ask, and it shall be given you; seek, and ye shall find; knock, and it shall be opened unto you:
> For every one that asketh receiveth; and he that seeketh findeth; and to him that knocketh it shall be opened.
>
> — MATTHEW 7:7-8

Go for it! He is waiting for you. Amen!

CHAPTER 9
TO WALK ON WATER, YOU MUST STEP OUT OF THE BOAT

When my family migrated to America in 1980, we settled in New York. We all lived within driving distance of each other. We went to school, went to church, bought houses, and worked in the City. I have said many times in the past to people who asked if I would ever leave New York to live in another state, and my answer was always, "No way." I loved it here so much that I couldn't fathom being anywhere else. I didn't care who moved; I wasn't going anywhere because there was no place like New York. I had worked in the City for decades, and all of my life revolved around it.

It's amazing how we can be so stuck in our ways, mindset, emotions, way of life, thinking, and where we live that we miss out on the vast world around us. Sometimes, it seems not even God can move us. For me, this all changed after my encounter with the Lord. As I pursued His presence, things didn't seem to have a hold on my heart anymore. I opened my eyes and heart to all that God had for me. My job, where I lived, and the City were losing their grip on me. My heart was free to be what He wanted me to be, to do what He wanted me to do, and to go where He wanted me to go. The words of a famous hymn say, "And the things of earth will grow strangely dim in the light of His glory and grace." This is exactly what was happening to me. Everything and everyone that seemed to hold me captive was being released, and I felt as free as a bird, ready to soar as high as I wanted.

One great lesson I learned is this: prayer, the Word, and fasting will change your life. As you pursue God's presence, your heart and mind are being renewed. Without trying to make anything happen, God will lead you, give you direction for your life, speak to you, open doors for you, and provide for you. His voice becomes clear, and you now know it's Him and quickly obey when He tells you to do something or go somewhere. Many are stuck in their Christian life due to a lack of prayer or time in the Word. There is no joy, no excitement, no souls won to the kingdom, no progress—just the same old life for decades.

> Now to Him who is able to [carry out His purpose and] do superabundantly more than all that we dare ask or think [infinitely beyond our greatest prayers, hopes, or dreams], according to His power that is at work within us.
>
> — EPHESIANS 3:20 (AMP)

Can you imagine that God is willing to do for you more than you can ask, dream, or even think? No one should remain the same when the Scripture admonishes us to move forward from glory to glory.

He will give you new thinking, new desires, new goals, new friends, and a new location. When the mind of Christ is formed in you, everything will change.

> Let this mind be in you, which was also in Christ Jesus.
>
> — PHILIPPIANS 2:5

This is what prayer does: it brings you closer to God, where you can hear His voice and His heartbeat. All your desires will change to align with His. Please don't waste your life on the mundane. If you get desperate and seek His face, your life will change for the better. It doesn't matter how old or young you are, whether you are in ministry or not, or whether you have any gifts or talents. God will bring out in you all He created you to be. It's not about whether you have an education or not—God is willing to use each one of us for His glory. You can live a beautiful life when you live it for God the way you were created to and be all that He created you to be.

One day in 2003, I was traveling home on the Staten Island Ferry when the Lord spoke to me to leave NYC and go to Florida. It was a still, small voice, like when He spoke to Elijah. I was shocked, as I had never considered this before. I quickly wrote it in my journal and prayerfully pondered what this would mean. Three months later, I resigned from my job with Lehman Brothers, gave up everything, and left. By then, nothing of the City had any hold on me. It was easy to say "Yes" to the Lord. I felt like Abraham when God told him to leave his country.

> Now the Lord had said unto Abram, Get thee out of thy country, and from thy kindred, and from thy father's house, unto a land that I will shew thee.
>
> — GENESIS 12:1

In a small way, I understand what God asked Abraham to do, and it's not easy. But obedience is better than sacrifice. I was willing to step out of the boat (out of the familiar and comfort zone) and plunge into the unknown so I could walk on water (experience the supernatural). I knew that if I sank, the Lord would rescue me. I had made up my mind, set my eyes like a flint, and there was no turning back. I could only go forward with God.

> For the Lord God will help me; therefore shall I not be confounded: therefore have I set my face like a flint, and I know that I shall not be ashamed.
>
> — ISAIAH 50:7

I arrived in Florida on a spiritual high with the fire of God burning in my belly. I began to ask the Lord to lead me to a church where people were hungry and desperate for Him. The Lord led me to a community church that met in an elementary school. I began attending and soon became part of that church, serving in many areas. We met for prayer often, and I never missed a prayer meeting. Since I now worked for myself from a home office, I had more time for prayer, the Word, and fasting. People who are retired or at home, whether by choice or not, should make good use of this time. This season should be used to seek God, read, and study His Word. Even if you were let go from a job, use this time wisely. You will find that God has given you this time off for a purpose. In the meantime, He will provide for you and give you a better job. Trust Him. No time in our lives is downtime; we should redeem the time, making the most of it while we are alive.

After one year, I became the Director of the Prayer Ministry. Our church was asked to lead the prayer at Christian events all over Orlando. I remember when Luis Palau held a festival in the Amway

Center. They asked us to mobilize 573 churches from all types of denominations to pray for the event. It was the first time in my life that I spoke to pastors and leaders from so many different churches. The Lord used this event to break down the walls of denominations in my heart and instead put His love in me for all people. As word got around about our church being a praying church, the Orlando Police Department (OPD) asked us to join them in praying against the crimes in many areas of the city.

One area, not far from downtown, had a reputation for murder and all types of crime. We walked on the land, prayed, and bound every principality and power of Hell in that community. The report came back that crime was almost nonexistent in the area after prayer. Once, the chaplain of the OPD attended a revival meeting we were in and asked my pastor for me. He came into the sanctuary where I was and asked me to pray for him. I thought, "Why me? My pastor is here." He took both my hands, placed them on his head, and said, "Pray for me." He wanted the anointing of the Holy Ghost in his life. He would join us many times as we prayed around the city to see people saved and crime drop.

For a season, six women met from midnight to 6 a.m. for prayer from Monday to Friday.

> But we will give ourselves continually to prayer, and to the ministry of the word.
>
> — ACTS 6:4

We witnessed many breakthroughs, healings, and deliverances. One night, one of the women who had been abused as a child was delivered from all past hurt and pain. God was moving in our lives as we set ourselves apart for Him.

At our church, many times, brethren from Uganda, who only added kerosene to the small fire burning in our hearts for revival, joined us. One day, I mentioned to the pastor from Uganda that someday I would love to visit Prayer Mountain in Kampala. He said, "You will." I didn't know that two months later, I would have one of the greatest experiences of my life, being with people who know how to worship and pray. Fifteen of us, including our pastor, attended a prayer conference in Kampala in 2004. We had three services per day, and every time felt like the first time for the people there. I had not experienced worship like that before. "How come they don't seem tired? How come they are joyful and worshipping the Lord with such enthusiasm for every service?" This spoke to me.

We spent three days on Prayer Mountain. One day, we had to select a section of the mountain to pray and spend time with the Lord. I found my spot to pray under a tree. This is East Africa, and as I stood under my tree and looked out, I realized I was very far from home. I couldn't believe I was in Africa. I never dreamed that I would travel anywhere. All I was doing was seeking God, and He was opening the world to me. Before I left, some young women, about twenty years old, asked if they could pray for me. I told them, "Yes, please pray for me." They laid their hands on my belly and prayed like I had never heard before. They prayed that out of the depth of my soul would come deep praise unto God. Everyone, from young to old, seemed to know how to pray and get hold of God. I felt blessed.

When they declared a fast for ninety days, one hundred percent of the people participated. No wonder they experienced more miracles, salvation, and revival in their church and land. I found the people there very hungry for the presence of God, and they pressed in hard. They were not lazy to pray or read the Word. Even in fasting, they committed themselves completely to seeking the Lord. We returned home with a greater fire burning in our hearts to see revival in our church, community, and souls getting saved. The Lord is doing in me and for me more than I could ever ask, dream, or think. Don't stay where you are if you want to go deeper; be willing to step out of the boat.

CHAPTER 10
DEEP CALLETH TO DEEP

> Deep calleth unto deep at the noise of thy waterspouts: all thy waves and thy billows are gone over me.
>
> — PSALM 42:7

My soul is stirred to a point and depth that I have not experienced before. I sense a breakthrough in my spirit as *"deep calleth unto deep."* Like the writer of the Psalms, my soul longs for God as in a dry and thirsty land, and I cry out to Him day and night. I feel like my soul will never be content here on earth. The more of His presence I experience, the more empty I feel and the more I want. God is infinite, and you realize how vast and great He is as you get closer to Him. During this time, I continued to press hard in prayer.

The Lord will connect you with people who will help you get to the next level. During my journey, one of those people was Pastor John from Uganda. He prays fervently, serves humbly as a servant of God, maintains integrity, loves Jesus, and serves as an apostle in the world. Whenever he visited our church, we eagerly sat in every service, prayer meeting, and teaching to receive all that God had for us. I was like a sponge, soaking up every word he preached. It was like cold water in a desert heat. The more time we spent with him, the more challenged we were to go deeper into the things of God. Pastor John impacted my walk with the Lord more than any other pastor I had known. He poured kerosene on a small flame and made it a bigger fire.

I experienced a mind-blowing introduction to some books for the first time. The Lord will not bring certain things your way until you are ready to receive them. The Lord has so many blessings for His people, but many cannot receive them. Whether it's spiritual, material, or financial blessings, we must position ourselves to not only receive them but also earn the trust to handle them. For example, if I am not faithful with thirty thousand dollars, how can God trust me with a million dollars? I must admit, the things, places, and blessings the Lord brought to me these past few years—I wasn't ready for them ten years ago. We must position ourselves in surrender, commitment, and consecration to the Lord so He can bless and use us.

You've heard the saying, "Hunger begets hunger," "Fire begets fire," and so on. The more time you spend around people with spiritual hunger, the more it gets on you, especially if that's your desire. My desire is not only to see revival in my lifetime but to be part and carrier of it. I want to light the flame in others as I journey along on this earth. It became necessary for me not only to pray, study the Word, and fast but also to surround myself with people of like passion and to read books that would fan the flame in my heart.

When I was elected as Director of the Prayer Ministries at my church, my pastor gave me Rees Howells' book *Intercessor* to read. I was delighted to have it until I began reading it. I thought, *Does my pastor know what this book is saying?* I am in no way capable of doing anything Rees Howells did. The book blew my mind as I had never thought people could live such a life as an intercessor, where God would ask you to do such difficult things. Rees came to a place where his will no longer existed—only the will of God. I faced the challenge of going deeper in my consecration and praying, "Not my will, but Thine be done."

Another book that impacted me was Hannah Whittall Smith's *The Christian's Secret of a Happy Life*. As I read the chronology of her life, I thought the title was inaccurate because nothing in her life spoke of happiness. It was one tragedy after another. Her children were dying, her husband was unfaithful, and many other difficulties occurred in her life. As I read on, the message became clear to me that despite all the problems and troubles in this life, we can be happy in Jesus because of our faith and trust in Him. I learned how to trust God more in difficult situations, and my faith became stronger. This book will challenge any Christian to examine their heart and to see where they stand in their faith in God. If you are not a serious Christian, don't even try to read either of these books because they will not make sense to you. But if you desire more and more of God and want to know Him in a deeper way, I say get these books quickly and devour them.

I never thought a Baptist would impact my life, but Henry Blackaby's book *Experiencing God* was a tremendous study for me. I had never heard of him before, and when this study introduced me to him, I didn't focus on his denomination but on the book's content. The Lord spoke to me through this book, telling me to not seek ministry. He said, "Seek My face to know Me, and I will bring the ministry." I grabbed this and ran with it like a lion was chasing me. It came at a pivotal time in my life as I sought the Lord for where He wanted me to serve. In my prayer, I stopped asking the Lord about ministry and instead said, "Lord, I want to know You more. Teach me Your ways and give me Your heart." Before I knew it, the Lord opened the door for the ministry He had for me.

Pastor John wrote many books, but two that impacted me the most were *Set Apart for God* and *Transforming Your World*. They spoke to my soul, and I began to see more clearly God's hand leading me. His many teachings, preaching on prayer altars, and fasting only ignited the fire in my belly to seek after God more. At the right time, God will bring the right people into your life who will be instrumental in taking you where you need to go next. It is never one person but many. Some will be with you for a season and then move on. Others may be around longer, but they too, may move on because it's time for new people in your new season. Don't be despondent when people leave you because God is fixing to take you further and deeper, which will require fresh fire from other people. Say amen!

One of my desires was to have a mentor. In prayer, I was very specific with the Lord about the kind of person I wanted as a mentor. She must be between the ages of sixty to seventy-five years old. She must be Spirit-filled, love God, and care for the younger generation of women to pour into them. When the Lord opened the door for me to work at the Super Channel Christian TV station, we would meet every Tuesday morning for prayer. There, I met the owner's wife, a woman of prayer, and I thought she must be the one. She fit all the criteria, but she was not the one. After meeting many women and hoping they would mentor me, I became discouraged and stopped looking or asking God for a mentor. What the Lord did instead was make me become that person to younger women. I took some younger and older women under my wings, taught them the Word of God, and led them in prayer. We met weekly for Bible study and prayer. These women became strong in faith and prayer.

Without realizing it, I no longer desired a mentor—I had become one.

Be careful what you ask for in prayer because God might just make you the answer to someone else's prayer for the same thing. I realized that the qualities I desired in someone else should be present in me. But am I willing to surrender my all to the Lord to break, mold, and make me into a vessel fit for His use? I remember how freeing it felt not to look to someone else or wait for someone else to fulfill my heart's desire when God is enough! All that we will ever need or desire can be found in Jesus. I never prayed for a mentor again and never will. I fulfilled the desire in my heart by doing it for someone else. Amen!

> The Lord is the portion of my inheritance, my cup
> [He is all I need] …
>
> — PSALM 16:5 (AMP)

Of all the books I have read, the Bible has had the greatest impact on my life from my teenage years until now. As I read and read and read, the Holy Spirit would speak to me. How many of you have experienced times when the Word became *sweet* to you? I have had that many times when it seemed like I could not get enough. Because the Word of God is alive, it speaks to us and changes us. Many verses and sections have had a profound effect on my Christianity. I believe this: if God said it, I believe it, and that settles it. I don't need to argue or analyze it. I love the childlike faith that Jesus said we should have. The story of Hannah in 1 Samuel chapter 1 spoke to me deeply. The first message I ever preached from a pulpit was from this text on desperate prayer. Nowhere have I seen a desperate prayer like that of Hannah. Perhaps I identified with Hannah in some way, as I have experienced times when there were "no words" to express to God how I felt or what I needed in prayer but only a groan.

> Likewise the Spirit also helpeth our infirmities: for we know not what we should pray for as we ought: but the Spirit itself maketh intercession for us with groanings which cannot be uttered.
>
> — ROMANS 8:26

I am thankful for the Holy Spirit.

I have many favorite verses throughout the Bible, but this verse transformed my life:

> But seek ye first the kingdom of God, and his righteousness; and all these things shall be added unto you.
>
> — MATTHEW 6:33

We were in a Panera Bread restaurant doing Bible study when the Lord exploded the revelation of this verse to me. During this time, I asked the Lord to teach me to give everything to Him—my life, future, finances, everything. This was a verse I had known since Sunday school, but I had never received such a revelation before. When He made it clear that all I needed to do was put Him first, make Him my primary concern, and He would take care of everything that concerned me, I jumped up, rejoicing. I got it—I really got it! It was difficult to let go of everything, give up control of every aspect of life, and trust God. It felt like a free fall or what I called a "bungee jump of faith," knowing that if I fell or crash-landed, He would catch me.

When you receive a revelation from the Lord, it will change your life. My entire outlook on life changed. It became a walk of faith, not a life of worry about tomorrow. Sometimes, we may think we have faith or trust God, but when everything is taken away, we will truly know if we have faith in Him or trust Him. Getting this revelation was the most freeing thing I have ever experienced. It is not head knowledge but spirit-to-spirit bearing witness. It is deep in your heart and soul; you feel and know it. Trying to explain it to someone else does not mean they will get it like you did. We preach and teach so people will hear the Word and grow in their faith, but nothing can replace your personal experience and revelation with God. I understand now when I listen to great men and women of God who had great encounters, they encourage people. Some people will hear but not get it, while others will take it and run with it. It's all about your heart and timing. I am reminded of the verse, *"They that hunger and thirst after righteousness shall be filled"* (Matthew 5:6). If this is you, everything you do will bring you to this place of fulfillment. God will lead you. He will direct you. He will guide you. He will put the right people in your path, and He will provide all you need. He is faithful to His Word. Trust Him!

There are times when I wonder, *Can I go any deeper?* I have been pressing in with prayer, fasting, studying the Word, serving faithfully, and experiencing the joy of the Lord. God is so vast, so great, and so majestic that we cannot grasp all of Him on this earth, even if we lived a thousand lifetimes. He is infinite. Our human minds cannot conceive His greatness. That is why the more we experience His presence and see signs and wonders, the more our hearts long for greater things. The revival at my kitchen table was a great and unique experience, but I want more. God desires to take us from glory to glory. Who knows if you were born for such a time as this? One of my prayers has been, *Lord, I want to fulfill my purpose on earth, the reason you allowed me to be born at this time, in this generation. I want to be and do all You created me for.* I will press forward hard until I fulfill all of Your plans and purposes for my life in my lifetime. I have made up my mind that where He leads me, I will follow. I strongly believe He has a purpose for my life, as well as for every person born into this world. It's up to each one to draw near to God and find that purpose, and once you do, run with it like there's no tomorrow.

CHAPTER 11
THE TIDE IS TURNING

> Now to Him who is able to [carry out His purpose and] do superabundantly more than all that we dare ask or think [infinitely beyond our greatest prayers, hopes, or dreams], according to His power that is at work within us.
>
> — EPHESIANS 3:20 (AMP)

Wow! Can you believe that God is willing to do more in your life than you ask, dream, or even think? This is mind-blowing for me. I have not been around Christians who believe for great things. Some think it's wrong to ask God for things beyond their ability or resources. I love God, and my only desire is to serve Him. I am okay leading the man at the gas station or the taxi driver to Christ. I never prayed or asked for big ministry or great things. But, like the Word says, He will do more than we can even dream.

When I lived in Florida, I knew in my spirit it was not permanent but for a season. I didn't know how long the season would last, but I knew it would end. Where I would be next was unknown, but I had learned to trust the Holy Ghost in me. While there, I went all out for the Lord with my church. We prayed, served, and shared the gospel at every opportunity. Six months after I became part of the church, the Lord spoke to me to help "build the church." I thought it was all financial. I told the Lord I didn't have money, so how could I help build the church? Anyway, from my home business, I tithed and gave more toward the land that was purchased so we could eventually build a church on that property. I sensed that it wasn't only financial but spiritual. As I led the Prayer Ministry and prayed with the believers, the Lord showed me that it was also to help build prayer in this church. Our Prayer Team and Ministry were strong as we gave ourselves to constant intercessory prayer and the Word. Do you know that when you pray, you become strong spiritually? Amen! You teach people to pray by praying, and when they hear you pray, they will learn to pray. I have experienced this. One young girl who was new to the church became a prayer warrior just by being with us and joining us in prayer. You become like who you hang around.

Not only did I go all out for the Lord with my church, but I also went hard after God in my personal life.

> My soul followeth hard after thee: thy right hand upholdeth me.
>
> — PSALM 63:8

I prayed hard, often, long, in the Spirit and with understanding. As I prayed, I could hear His voice more clearly, was strengthened spiritually, had more discernment, and became much more aware in both the Spirit and the natural. Next was the Word. I devoured it cover to cover many times. So often, He would speak to me through His Word, and my life would change. My faith grew, and I could see more clearly each day. The Word became sweet, fulfilling, satisfying, and strengthening. Finally, I fasted regularly, often only on water. I did 40 days, 21 days, 10 days, 7 days, 3 days, and even 1-day fasts. This was personal, apart from fasting with my church. As I persevered and ran hard after God, these three things—prayer, the Word, and fasting—became foundational in my life and Christian journey. If you practice these things, your life will never be the same. God will take you to heights you never dreamed of, places you never thought you would go, and connect you with all the right people you didn't even ask for.

After about six years, I began to feel restlessness in my spirit. I didn't understand it then, but later, it became clear that the Lord was moving me back to New York.

> Oh, the depth of the riches and wisdom and knowledge of God! How unsearchable are His judgments and decisions and how unfathomable and untraceable are His ways!
>
> — ROMANS 11:33 (AMP)

God's ways are not like our ways, so we must learn to trust Him at all times. He will never harm us but only has the best for us as a good Father does. This next move or chapter of my life didn't come without trials. My church actually came against me. My pastor thought I wanted to do my own thing and even take over his church. That was far from my mind because I knew since I was fifteen years old that the Lord had called me to be an evangelist.

Let me share the event that made it clear the Lord was leading me. Remember Romans 8:28 says, *"And we know that all things work together for good to them that love God, to them who are the called according to his purpose."* For the believer, there are no situations in our lives that God will not use for His glory and our good. When God is in control of your life and future, you can totally trust Him for a good outcome. We must believe the Word!

Our pastor asked us to start Bible studies in our homes. We had many groups started: the Men's Group, Women's Group, Youth Group, and others. I didn't want to start a Bible study at my home. My excuse was that I had a dog. But I felt something in my belly to do something for the Lord, though I didn't know what it was. I went on my first forty-day fast to hear from the Lord and get clarity. At the end of the fast, in a Walmart parking lot, the Lord spoke to me about starting a Women's Bible Study at my home. The next week, I mentioned it to some of the women, and we started to meet on Saturday evenings at 6 p.m. Six women attended regularly. This wasn't a normal Women's Bible Study, for the Lord spoke to me to "care for their souls" and to love them. It was deep in my spirit. When we met, I would teach the Word, pray, and worship. Many of the women stayed until midnight because the presence of the Lord was so mighty among us. Some stayed until 2 a.m. I remember the night when joy broke out, and we began to worship and sing. One of the women, who lived in my neighborhood was ninety years old. She was Catholic but got saved and liked to be with us. The night when joy broke out, I watched her walk to her home one block away, singing with the joy of the Lord bubbling out of her. She didn't care that it was late. She had never before experienced the presence of the Lord and such joy like this. Oh, how it blessed my heart to watch her come to know Jesus at her age.

Before the Bible study started, the Lord spoke to me and said, "Can I trust you with the details of people's lives?" He took me through a process to prepare me because many women would share deep, painful, personal things in their lives. This began to happen as the women felt safe to open up and share some of the most personal things that either happened to them or they were experiencing—

things like abortion, rape, abuse, and marital problems. We prayed together and saw many healed of past hurt or delivered from various bondages and strongholds from childhood. The power of God set many of the women free. The women shared things at this Bible study that they had never shared with anyone before. Now, I saw what the Lord was doing as He prepared me to hold in confidence the personal stories of His precious daughters. I could say, "Yes, Lord, You can trust me." It was my honor and joy to serve the Lord by being a blessing to His children. Many of the women, even years later, testified that their lives were forever changed as they experienced the teachings of the Word of God. They couldn't wait for Saturday nights. Some drove long distances to come, but like they said, "It was worth it."

I was so excited to share this with our pastor, who was out of the country at the time. I couldn't wait to meet with him to share the good news of what the Lord had done when he returned. However, in the meantime, some of the women I was very close with, those I prayed with, broke bread with, and served with, called our pastor while he was abroad and told him how I had stepped out and was doing my own thing. When he returned, we met, but instead of sharing the exciting news that I had finally said "yes" to leading a Bible study, I received a scolding. I couldn't believe my ears. I felt hurt and like an outcast. For a few months, I was churchless. I felt betrayed by both my pastor and the women I was close with. I began to worship at other churches. Once, I even went to a Baptist church, and I was the only one lifting my hands to worship the Lord. I didn't care how the others worshiped. They were singing some of the most beautiful hymns that I love, and I wasn't going to sit with my hands folded.

One day, while praying and asking the Lord why this happened, He spoke to me that it was time to return because He had plans for my life. Sometimes, the Lord has to almost hit me in the face for me to "get it," or He has to put a huge roadblock in front of me to get my attention to turn the other way. Maybe I'm a bit stubborn like Jonah, who had to be swallowed by a whale before he "got it" and said, "Okay, Lord, I'll do what You want me to do and go where You want me to go." I realized later that what people did to me, God would use to propel me into the destiny and future He had for me. You may be going through betrayal from people around you, whether inside or outside the church. When this happens, look up, get ready, and prepare yourself because God is about to step in and move you forward. No bad situation will be in vain when you trust the Lord with it. He will bring good out of it.

> As for you, you meant evil against me, but God meant it for good in order to bring about this present outcome, that many people would be kept alive ...
>
> — GENESIS 50:20 (AMP)

The Scripture is clear that all things will work together for the good of those who love God and are called according to His purpose. If the people who turned against me only knew that God would flip this thing for my good, they would change their minds. Destiny was awaiting me. God had great plans for my life, and no one—not even the Devil in Hell—could stop Him. It's like a caterpillar undergoing a transformation or "metamorphosis" before a beautiful butterfly emerges. There is a process and a struggle from the egg to the larva to the pupa, and finally, to something beautiful we can admire in the adult butterfly. You, too, will have to go through some painful situations in life. But when you emerge, you will be a vessel of honor, fit for the Master's use. It doesn't matter if someone rejected you, blamed you, hated you, put you to shame, or left you to die—those whom God uses greatly are those who suffer greatly. Please hear this in your spirit. If you are such a person, get ready because God is about to flip the switch on the enemy of your soul and take you where you've never been before. Joseph was such a person. Joseph faced hatred, being left for dead, being despised, being sold, being accused, and being imprisoned—but God was with him. In due season, God elevated him and made him a great blessing. Thank God for the people who did you wrong because, as a child of God, "all things will work together for your good and God's glory." God will flip the situation.

> None of the rulers of this age recognized and understood this wisdom; for if they had, they would not have crucified the Lord of glory.
>
> — 1 CORINTHIANS 2:8 (AMP)

Can you imagine if the Roman governor, Pontius Pilate, only knew that Jesus would rise from the grave on the third day and His fame would spread not only across Rome but the entire world? He probably would not have ordered the crucifixion of Jesus Christ. What the enemy meant for bad, God will always turn around for good. They spat on Jesus, called Him Beelzebub, mocked Him, rejected Him, chose a murderer instead, and hung Him on a cross to die a cruel death. They thought they had won, but Easter morning was coming, and their plans would be foiled. God is always ahead of the enemy and always has a plan. We can trust Him when we can't see ahead—it's called faith.

The darkest hour is always before daybreak. If you stay the course, your breakthrough will come. God will not fail or disappoint you. People will fail and disappoint you, but God never will. His Word is firm, His promises are true, and He is faithful.

> For we are His workmanship [His own master work, a work of art], created in Christ Jesus [reborn from above—spiritually transformed, renewed, ready to be used] for good works, which God prepared [for us] beforehand [taking paths which He set], so that we would walk in them [living the good life which He prearranged and made ready for us].
>
> — EPHESIANS 2:10 (AMP)

God will use every situation in our lives to make us His masterpiece. His plans for us are greater than what we desire for ourselves. Like the pain of birthing a child, so too is the pain of birthing destiny. It's the pain and hard times that perfect the things in us that God will use. In every situation we go through, there is a lesson to learn that will have eternal value and impact. Do not despise the hard times, the lonely times, the sad times—for in the dark place, new life is birthed.

God is about to take me to heights I never dreamed of, depths I didn't know existed, and places I couldn't imagine. To get there, I had to go through the hard places, rejection, and loneliness, and be willing to embrace change. I have learned to trust the God who saved me to take me where I don't know and to do in me what I am not capable of doing. Amen!

CHAPTER 12
BACK INTO THE UNKNOWN

I am not the same person I was when I left New York. I have been in the presence of God, and in His presence, we are changed. I have been on the mountaintop and caught a glimpse of His glory that marked me forever. There is no fear of the unknown because I know I can trust Him where He leads me. All I have to do is follow.

My first thought was to find the right church. I had been a member of a few churches here, but that was not where I desired to be in this season. I began to pray and ask the Lord to show me a church where there is "Godly Leadership" to which I can wholeheartedly submit. Being around the church for most of my life, I had seen all kinds of leadership, and many did not line up with the Word of God. We need leadership we can trust, leadership that loves the people like God loves His people, and leadership that has integrity, godliness, and holiness. Too many are concerned with control, money, and numbers but do not care for the sheep.

Here are some strong words God has for pastors and leaders. Read it and weep:

> Son of man, prophesy against the shepherds of Israel, prophesy, and say unto them, Thus saith the Lord God unto the shepherds; Woe be to the shepherds of Israel that do feed themselves! should not the shepherds feed the flocks?
>
> — EZEKIEL 34:2

> Thus saith the Lord God; Behold, I am against the shepherds; and I will require my flock at their hand, and cause them to cease from feeding the flock; neither shall the shepherds feed themselves any more; for I will deliver my flock from their mouth, that they may not be meat for them.
>
> — EZEKIEL 34:10

In prayer, I said to the Lord that I am willing to drive the distance to be in the right church. I cannot settle for mediocrity as a Christian or be in a cold, dead church. I want to be with people who love God, people who are desperate, hungry, praying, and living holy lives before God. I understand there is no perfect church, but there are pastors and leaders who are after God's heart. That's where I want to be. I have come too far, gone through too much, to settle for anything less than the best.

The Lord spoke to me about Times Square Church. Now, this was a surprise as I only thought of Manhattan as a place where people work, not go to church. I knew about the church but never thought much of it. But the Lord knew where I needed to be at this time, so He led me there. Being in ministry is not always easy to be in the pew, but it was the place for me for this season. The presence of God was there. Pastor David Wilkerson spoke the Word to our souls. He stirred us to live holy and serve God. I went to three services every Sunday, Bible study on Wednesdays, and prayer meetings on Thursdays at that time.

On Sundays, I called it "The Marathon." My friends and I would go to the 10 a.m. service and then have lunch in Central Park. We would return for the 3 p.m. service and then go to Starbucks for coffee afterward. At 6 p.m., we returned for the evening evangelistic service and then drove across the East River to go home. I got filled up with the Word even more. It was exciting to be in TSC and experience the presence of God with the people of God. When you are desperate for God and His presence, distance doesn't matter, cost doesn't matter, time doesn't matter, the length of service doesn't matter, and going to church every day, if possible, is a joy and privilege. You find you have the energy and strength because the Holy Ghost quickens our physical bodies, and everything comes alive in His presence. All you want is more and more of Him!

After six months in the 10 a.m. service, the Lord spoke to me to give up my seat and step into ministry. I began to inquire and found out there is a ministry called "Prayer During the Preaching." I signed up for the classes and went through the vetting process. I appreciated this process because, in many churches, people serve in ministry who are not living right and should not be serving in some areas. This told me how serious TSC is about the Church and Ministry of Jesus Christ. The church had to vet you spiritually and morally, regardless of the ministry you were in.

After the training was over, I joined fifty other believers under the pulpit to pray while the pastor was preaching. When I first saw this, I was impressed by the number of people praying during the preaching for every service, but I found out that this wasn't a large number when you consider the size of the church. Yet still, I had never seen that before. People across the world watch the services online and receive blessings. I have heard people in the USA talk about how anointed that church is with a rich presence of God. That is because of the prayer. You cannot see what goes on underground with the prayer and spiritual warfare being fought for the people in the sanctuary and those listening while the preaching is going on, but you can see the outcome and fruits of it. Prayer is the key to success in any ministry.

About one thousand people attended the Thursday night prayer meeting. Many, like myself, attended after work. There is no tiredness in His presence. The joy of the Lord is our strength. Taking the train and then a bus after the prayer meeting, I would reach home at about 11 p.m., but there was no thought of how late it was. When you are consumed with God and His presence, it feels like time stands still as you move at a fast pace in the Spirit that the world around you is not aware of. As you are caught up in a heavenly pursuit, you almost seem oblivious to what is happening in the natural, physical world. When I was young and in Sunday school, we used to sing a chorus that said, "I am wrapped up, tied up, and tangled up in Jesus." That is me—I just want more of Jesus!

While serving at TSC, the Lord spoke to me to go to Bible school. Now, understand that I never asked the Lord for this. I began to pray as to where I should go, how I would pay for it, and when I would find time to attend school. The Lord led me to the Assemblies of God New York District School of Ministry. I made contact and found out that it was only 15 minutes from my home. Additionally, they held classes on Saturdays, and the tuition was affordable. It seemed too good to be true because it fit my schedule and budget perfectly. I registered and began attending classes.

I was learning a lot and enjoying studying with the other students. One day, while driving to class, it dawned on me that I didn't know why I was going to Bible school. All I knew was that the Lord said to go. If you had asked me why or what ministry plans I had, I would say, "I don't know." God told me to go, and I was just obeying Him. Whatever plans He has for me in the future, He will bring them to pass. To some, this may sound foolish. But to me, I was like a child obeying her father, and I would do what He told me to do. All I desired was to serve Him, and I didn't think I needed Bible school or a big ministry title to do so. But God had a plan for me that was bigger than my prayers or dreams. I didn't understand it, but one thing I was sure of was that I could trust Him completely. End of story!

I found out it was a three-year school that involved not only classroom study and exams but a practical ministry aspect too. I contacted TSC to inquire if they would recognize this and allow me to complete the practical aspect of my Christian education. However, they informed me they were not affiliated with the AG and could not accommodate my request. I didn't worry but placed it in God's hands and continued to serve in the Prayer Ministry and attend classes on Saturdays. When God calls us, He will fulfill that call. Where He leads us, He will provide. I had nothing to worry about because He was leading the way. All I was required to do was follow Him.

It was coming up on four years soon at TSC. I was enjoying the ministry I was in. I had made many friends here, and the Word was preached powerfully each time we came to church. But I was beginning to feel a restlessness in my heart, soul, and spirit, and I didn't know what it was. As I prayed and continued to cry out to God, I sensed it was time to pour out what He had poured into me. How do I do this? Could I make this happen? I had no clue.

During this time, I worked within walking distance of TSC. I came to know many women there, and as we fellowshipped together, they would share their stories and struggles, and we would pray together. There came a time when many of these women would make appointments with me during my lunch hour and meet me for coffee so they could share their hearts, and I could pray for them and encourage them. They would travel from nearby states like New Jersey and various boroughs in NYC. While TSC was a wonderful church and place to worship the Lord, it was difficult for people to meet and talk with a pastor. The process of getting an appointment was long and almost impossible. One woman who reached out for an appointment to get counsel for her marriage got divorced and never heard from the church. She mentioned later that maybe if she had received some counsel, her marriage could have been saved. This is the sad part of big churches. People are hurting and need a pastor to talk to, counsel them, and pray with them—not a pastor who is whisked away after service by security guards. Church is still about people, not programs, prestige, and position. Jesus made time for people. He came to save people, not buildings. *For the Son of man is come to seek and to save that which was lost* (Luke 19:10), and Ezekiel 34 is a stark warning to the shepherds today. Take heed!

CHAPTER 13
CROSSING THE EAST RIVER

The stirring and restlessness in my spirit became more and more intense. It felt like a caterpillar in a cocoon that wants to get out. What do you do when you are feeling like this? You pray, pray, and pray. I continued to pray and cry out to the Lord. It felt like change was coming, but I had no clue from which direction. It seemed like my time at Times Square Church (TSC) was coming to a completion. I had fulfilled my assignment there, and it was time for the next assignment. I didn't know what, where, how, who, or when—but again, if there's one thing I've learned in this life with God, it's how to trust Him. King Solomon reminds us:

> Trust in the Lord with all thine heart; and lean not
> unto thine own understanding.
>
> — PROVERBS 3:5

During prayer one day, the Lord spoke to me that it was time to "Cross over the East River," which meant it was time to leave TSC and serve somewhere else. I honestly didn't know where to go, so, as we are supposed to do, I prayed and waited on the Lord. I didn't mention this to anyone, but kept it in my heart before the Lord daily in prayer.

There are things the Lord speaks to us that we should be careful about when and with whom we share them. Not everyone in your circle is on the same path as you or has your best interests in their heart.

> But Mary treasured up all these things and pondered them in her heart.
>
> — LUKE 2:19 (NIV)

She did not need to announce this good news to the world—God did it His way. Remember, too, that the Devil does not know the future, and once he hears it from your lips, he will try to sabotage the plans God has for you. So, be wise as a serpent and harmless as a dove (Matthew 10:16). Know when to be quiet and when to speak. Not everything God speaks to you personally needs to be shared openly with everyone. There is a right time, and there are the right people you can trust who can bear up what you share in prayer. Not everyone will be happy for you, and not everyone loves you. We all were born with a fallen nature. Remember that and be discerning in all you say, to whom you say it, and when you say it.

> For my thoughts are not your thoughts, neither are your ways my ways, saith the Lord.
> For as the heavens are higher than the earth, so are my ways higher than your ways, and my thoughts than your thoughts.
>
> — ISAIAH 55:8-9

The Lord's timing is perfect, and we can trust Him to guide us. I often say, "The Lord comes to me from left field"—from unexpected angles my mind could not conceive. In our attempts to understand God, we will always miss the mark. We must walk by faith and fully trust His guidance because He is beyond our understanding. The Apostle Paul describes our great God:

> Oh, the depth of the riches and wisdom and knowledge of God! How unsearchable are His judgments and decisions and how unfathomable and untraceable are His ways!
>
> — ROMANS 11:33 (AMP)

I knew the Lord was leading me, so there was no worry or fear about the future or ministry. I have always desired to serve the Lord and tell people about Him. I never asked for or desired big titles—or any title, for that matter. Whether it was sharing the gospel on the street, the subway, the gas station, or in a taxi, I was willing. I never thought of the pulpit or a big stage. But the plans God has for us are greater than what we have for ourselves. He is a big God with big plans for us, and if we surrender our all to Him, He will do in and through us more than we are capable of—more than our prayers or dreams.

> Now to Him who is able to [carry out His purpose and] do superabundantly more than all that we dare ask or think [infinitely beyond our greatest prayers, hopes, or dreams], according to His power that is at work within us.
>
> — EPHESIANS 3:20 (AMP)

Many have missed their destiny because they didn't trust Him beyond their abilities. All God is looking for is an obedient, available vessel to pour His Spirit into and to do exploits in this world for His Kingdom.

One day, a friend came to join me for lunch in the city and mentioned that she had something to discuss with me. She stated that she had started a church and would like me to consider being the Associate Pastor. I knew this was the Lord because He had already spoken to me to "Cross the East River." I told her I would pray and get back to her. I had never considered pastoring, although I knew God had given me such a heart. As I prayed about this next assignment, the Lord said to trust Him to lead me and use me.

The following Sunday, I mentioned to my ministry elder and leader that the Lord was calling me to leave TSC and minister in Queens. I asked if he would anoint me and release me to accept this calling. In two months, my TSC prayer team anointed me, prayed for me, and released me. Leaving the team I had been with for four years was sad, but at the same time, I felt excited about the new season and all the Lord had for me. From glory to glory, step by step, He guides us. The Lord opened this door. I never asked Him to be a pastor. One of the things the Lord spoke to me many years ago was never to seek ministry. He said, "Seek me, and I will bring the ministry." I have lived that ever since and have seen the faithfulness of God in my life.

As I began to pastor, the Lord put a deep love in my heart for the people. As with every assignment the Lord has given me, I poured myself in and gave more than 100 percent. My aim was always to please the Lord. I preached once or twice per month, led prayer meetings, led women's ministry, taught Sunday school classes, and did administrative work (my least favorite thing in ministry). During this time, I worked full-time, attended Bible school on Saturdays, and did ministry work full-time. You may ask, "How can this be?" His grace is sufficient. When you are hungry and thirsty for God and His presence in your life, when you have surrendered your life, when you make God your primary concern and put Him first, there is nothing too much for the Lord or too much ministry. His joy becomes your strength, and as you obey and do what He tells you, He gives more and more grace.

I enjoyed working for the Lord and doing what He called me to do. Ministry was never a burden to me because *"My yoke is easy, and My burden is light"* (Matthew 11:30). When you depend on the Holy Spirit to do the work of the Lord in you, put your confidence in Him and not in your ability, be steadfast in prayer, and trust Him completely, you find that the burden is light and the journey is joyful. You can be happy serving the Lord if you learn to trust Him. Remember, it's *"not by might, nor by power, but by My Spirit, says the Lord"* (Zechariah 4:6). This is the secret to a happy, joyful, and successful ministry. God never calls us to do anything for Him in our strength, but He will equip us for the call and strengthen us for the work by His Spirit.

One of the joys of pastoring is seeing growth in the people. I remember the first time I baptized new converts. It was such a joyful occasion to witness and be part of this life-transforming ordinance of the church. This was the fruit of teaching the New Believers Class. My heart was happy to see young and old pursue their relationship and commitment to the Lord.

Prayer is the life source of the church and every individual believer. We have all heard the saying, "No prayer, no power; more prayer, more power"—this is a true saying. The person who prays will have the power to live a happy, fulfilled, and victorious Christian life. The church that prays will experience the power of God in signs, wonders, and miracles. Prayer will take a regular person who lives a regular Christian life and propel them into things they have never dreamed about. When we pray, we are changed from the inside out, and God begins to move in our hearts and lives in ways beyond our human comprehension. Prayer changes everything.

It will change our mindset and how we think. It will change our desires, dreams, and goals for our life. It will give a new direction. All of a sudden, you don't think the same anymore. You do not love the same things anymore. Everything is changing in you from the inside. While the world around you cannot see it yet, God is doing something deeper and greater in you. In His time, He will show you off to the world, and He will get all the glory. You are His masterpiece, and He delights in you.

When a church prays, it will be evident in the believers and the surrounding community. God will move when the church prays. There will be salvation, healing, signs, wonders, and miracles. There will also be a spirit of reverence and holiness toward God. This is the reason the enemy will fight prayer meetings. It is the reason that the prayer meeting, which is the most important meeting in the church, is the least attended. Why? The enemy knows that when we pray, we become powerful as the Spirit of God works in our lives. The enemy knows that when the church prays, God goes to work on their behalf, and he will be ineffective in his efforts to derail or render the church helpless.

A prayerless believer or church is only going through religious practices but lacks the power of God to overcome. Without prayer, your vision is limited, but with prayer, you have a panoramic view of life and this world. In other words, when you are connected to God, you gain a God-sized view. Prayer connects us to God and draws us so close that we hear His voice clearly.

It is said that prayer is synonymous with gas in your car. If you have no gas, it does not matter how pretty, expensive, or new your car is—you are not going anywhere. For the prayerless Christian, it does not matter how much you say you love the Lord or how committed you are to serving in your church spiritually, you are not moving forward or going anywhere. You will have no power to cast out the smallest demon in someone who comes your way. The Bible says we go from glory to glory. It is not intended for believers to remain stagnant in their relationship with God. Being a Christian is more than going to church every Sunday, Wednesday, or Friday. It is more than being involved in various ministries in your church. It is having an intimate relationship with God. You can only accomplish this through prayer. Think of Jesus and how much He prayed. If Jesus needed to pray, how much more do all of us who call ourselves Christians need to pray daily? Get back to prayer, lock yourself in your prayer closet, and let God discover you. Calling and ministry are birthed in His presence.

The prayerless church merely has religious services and does good works to pacify itself. Many churches spend more time planning programs than they spend praying. You can have the most beautiful cathedral or building but have no power. Even if you put on the best shows, concerts, and events, lives may still not be transformed. Church is not about entertainment but should be a house of prayer. I have witnessed taking unsaved people to church who want an encounter with God only to discover the church is more interested in entertaining and making people comfortable living in sin. They lower the lights, use strobe lights, take away the hymn books, and remove the pews to make the unsaved feel comfortable. This is what churches do when they do not pray. They will do everything to make the church look and feel like the world. The unsaved don't need that. They had that, and now they need God. When they come to church, they want to meet with God. There is absolutely no substitute for prayer or the presence of God in the church. Where there is prayer, there will be a demonstration of the power of God, and people will not only feel it but also experience transformation in their own lives. This is God's desire for His Church.

> It is written, My house is the house of prayer: but ye have made it a den of thieves.
>
> — LUKE 19:46

While pastoring, I continued to attend Bible school. Once you pass all exams and complete the practical requirements, you can be certified as a minister after the first year. During my first year, I went through the process and was now a "Certified Minister" with the Assemblies of God. I remember when one of our district leaders came to present me with my certificate and plaque as a "Minister of the Gospel." It was a proud moment. My mom and some other family members attended the service that day. It was surreal to me, as I never asked the Lord for this, but He led me to this point.

Not sure if I should pursue the next level to be a "Licensed Minister," I prayed and asked the Lord if I should continue. A clear "yes" came into my spirit, so I registered and continued with classes for the next year. It was a real joy to study the Word with the other students. Again, at this point, I didn't know what the Lord had in store for me, but I continued faithfully serving Him and being obedient to what He called me to at the present time. The Lord has given me great strength to work full-time, serve Him full-time in the church, and also go to school. The Holy Ghost is a quickening spirit. Not only do I repeat the verse that says, *"I can do all things through Christ who strengthens me"* (Philippians 4:13), but I was living out this verse of scripture.

After completing my second year in Bible school, passing all exams, and fulfilling all practical requirements, I was now a Licensed Minister. Praise the Lord! This was more than my mind could conceive. No one in my family has attained this. I often wonder why the Lord chose me. I am not gifted or talented in any way. All I know is that I love Jesus, and my only desire is to live a life pleasing in His sight and serve Him faithfully until He comes back or takes me home. That's it!

CHAPTER 14
RESTORATION OF THE CALL

> Call unto me, and I will answer thee, and show thee
> great and mighty things, which thou knowest not.
>
> —JEREMIAH 33:3

I believe the Word of God. I felt the call of the Evangelist before I even knew what an Evangelist was. After I got saved at Youth Camp and came back home after one week, I hit the streets and began to preach. The fire of God was burning in my heart to see the lost get saved. I had a clear revelation that the Lord is coming soon, and if people do not repent and turn to Jesus, they will end up in a lost eternity away from Him.

As I recall, most of my messages were on repentance, the coming of the Lord, and the urgency of the hour. It was the pure gospel. Today, many of our messages are on motivation, psychology, and living your best life now. We don't mention holiness much, and we don't preach about the coming of the Lord often, so people lack the motivation to live in a way that is holy and pleasing to God. They seem unaware that He is coming back soon and that they must stay in a place of readiness. After over forty years, His coming is now closer than when I first believed.

When I came to America, the focus shifted to getting an education and a good job. I had never worked before, but life was changing. I served the Lord in the Children's Ministry, but the call of the Evangelist was fading away from me. My greater focus was getting a college education and eventually finding a good job. I wonder how many of us have lost our focus and true calling along the way. I realize that when we don't maintain a consistent, fervent prayer life, our minds begin to sway with the world, and we lose our way. We still go to church and do ministry, but Jesus is no longer the focus. We have lost our first love, and as John said in Revelation 2:4, *"Nevertheless, I have somewhat against thee, because thou hast left thy first love."* When this happens to Christians, they just go through the motions of religion and don't even realize it. Other things begin to occupy our hearts, minds, and thoughts. We are drifting away and don't even know it. This happened to me. I loved Jesus with all my heart and served Him, but my focus was making a good life in America while serving the Lord. The desire to serve God as an Evangelist no longer existed in my heart.

During my encounter with the Lord at my kitchen table, from which this book was birthed, God started restoring my life, my joy, my song, and my calling. The greatest thing the Lord did in me during that encounter was to birth deep, travailing prayer as I had never seen or heard before. Day and night, I cried out to the Lord in prayer. It was not for anything material but *"that I may know you more each day"* and *"that you will use my life for your glory."* I believe that God has great plans for every one of us, but we miss them because we do not pray. It has nothing to do with your education or lack of it, nothing to do with where you were born or your family background.

> For the gifts and the calling of God are irrevocable
> [for He does not withdraw what He has given, nor
> does He change His mind about those to whom
> He gives His grace or to whom He sends His call].
>
> — ROMANS 11:29 (AMP)

He is waiting for us to come to Him, to seek Him with our whole hearts, so He may deposit in us all we need to fulfill our destiny and calling. I hope everyone who reads this book will hear me in their spirit. It was not until I began to pray that God began to bring back to me the prayer I prayed as a teenager, the calling I heard to be an Evangelist as a teenager. I began to weep as, for over two decades, I never thought of it. Actually, seeing ministry in America, I did not think I had what it takes to do it. The preachers I saw on television intimidated me. In no way, in the natural, did I think I even measured up. I didn't have what it takes. This is all thinking in the flesh. I am reminded that *"it is not by might nor by power, but by My Spirit,"* says the Lord. This Scripture in Zechariah 4:6 led me to total dependence on God. What did He call you to do that you think you are not qualified for? If you pray, seek His face, and totally surrender to His will, God will use you in a mighty way.

After being licensed as a Minister with the Assemblies of God, I wasn't sure if I should go to the next level for ordination. This was totally out of scope for me. This had never been a prayer point or desire of mine. So again, I prayed and asked the Lord if I should pursue this, and He said yes. It reminded me of when David prayed in 1 Samuel 30:8 and inquired of the Lord if he should pursue his enemies, and the Lord answered him to pursue, for he would overtake them and recover all he lost. I wonder what has kept you from pursuing the call of God on your life. Is it fear? I believe this is one of the biggest hindrances from the Devil against God's people fulfilling their destiny. Fear will keep you from accomplishing many things in life. It will keep you from stepping out to do great things for God or even in the world you live in.

There is a saying that fear and faith do not go hand in hand. Either you have one or the other. I came to realize that this is a true saying, for faith says, *"I can do all things through Christ who strengthens me."* This is more than a Bible verse; it is God's living, breathing word, and if we believe, then all things become possible. Our flesh, or natural man, always stands in the way of faith because faith does not make sense to our natural thinking. When we realize that all God has called us to do is not based on our strength or ability but His, then it makes all the difference in the world. As I continued to pursue Him, I found that my faith was getting stronger and stronger. I could believe God for things that were totally impossible. Soon, faith overcame all my fears, and now I can trust God and believe His word. Where He leads, I will follow.

In total obedience, I continued in Bible school for the final year and ordination. During this final year of study, my heart began to stir again. Many things that lay dormant in my heart and soul for decades were being awakened. I was reminded of Joel 2:25-26: *"And I will restore to you the years that the locust hath eaten, the cankerworm, and the caterpillar, and the palmerworm, my great army which I sent among you. And ye shall eat in plenty, and be satisfied, and praise the name of the Lord your God, that hath dealt wondrously with you: and my people shall never be ashamed."* It felt like every cell in my body, soul, and spirit was coming alive, and I could feel it literally. Things were changing in me. Faith was coming alive. Joy was coming alive. Peace was coming alive. Purpose was coming alive. The future was coming alive. God was doing a new thing, and I knew it very well. Once faith is alive in you, all things become possible, and you can conquer the world.

During this final year, the Lord began to speak to me again about the office of the Evangelist. He began to restore the call and desire. I would weep because it seemed that I had wasted many years. I would weep to think that God would use me. My heart was so humbled with gratitude to think that the Lord did not forget me or His call on my life at the age of fifteen. Soon, it became clear in my spirit that this would be the direction of my future. I was still pastoring, unsure how or when this would occur. When the Lord opened the door for me to pastor, it was clear in my spirit that it was for a season. I did not know how long the season would be, but I knew for sure He was leading me. As it became clear to me that I would be moving forward as an Evangelist, I kept it in my heart before the Lord in prayer. One thing I was confident and prayed fervently about was that the God who opened the door for me to pastor would also open this door as I stepped into this office of the Evangelist.

This was not something I shared with anyone privately or publicly. The first time I would open up and share this was during my district interview with the Presbyters before ordination. The interviewers asked me about my calling, and this was the very first time I spoke about the call of the Evangelist. Something broke in the Heavens when I shared this.

> Decree a thing, and it shall be established.
>
> —JOB 22:28

As I began to speak of it, it became more and more real to me. I felt that my time to step into my calling was coming soon. It was near, but I still didn't know when. I had learned to wait on the Lord and pray through until He answered and gave direction. I was getting excited about what the Lord was doing in my life. This had been my call and ministry, and that which I had lost was now being restored.

My greatest desire had been to fulfill the calling of the Lord on my life before I left this world. Nothing else mattered more to me. It wasn't just to be in ministry but to do what He had called me to do. Nothing would satisfy my heart more than to see God use my life to do what I was born to do. My prayer over many years had been that the Lord would use my life to impact my generation and fulfill His plan and purpose for which He had me born into this world at this time. Although I did ministry all my life, I felt something was missing. My heart was crying out for more—for destiny. I would reflect on my teenage years preaching on the street corner and ferry terminal with no title or fear but just pure love for the Lord and the gospel. How my heart ached for that again. My greatest joy is preaching; nothing else can give me greater joy or sense of purpose than doing what I was born to do.

During this final year of study, the Lord began to open doors for me to preach at other churches and Christian events. It seemed that He was affirming my call, and the time of my "stepping out of the boat and walking on water" was near. I remember preaching at a church on a Wednesday night, and on my way home, they called and asked me to preach again in two weeks on a Sunday. I thought this was too good to be true. It was surreal, but I was happy to be used by the Lord. I was also thankful that He was opening the doors and not man. I love it when the Lord does things in and through my life without me even asking Him. He is a faithful God in whom I have placed my entire hope, faith, and confidence. He can do anything but fail.

In prayer one day, the Lord gave me clear direction on when I would step into the role of Evangelist. Knowing this humbled me to the core. The enemy tried to bring fear into my heart, but knowing that I had heard from the Lord debunked all of Satan's lies and attempts to hold me down. I am reminded of Peter—if he had never stepped out of the boat, he would have never walked on water, and we would not be talking about him today. I want to step out and do great things for the Lord, and I know it will cost me. I am willing to pay the price, whatever it is. At the end of my life, I never want to say, "I wish I had said yes to the Lord," "I wish I had done this or that," or "I wish I had stepped out in faith and trusted God." I don't want that to be the final chapter of my life. I want to know that I have answered when He called and did what He called me to do. I want no regrets.

I completed Bible school and was heading to ordination. My ordination service was beautiful and impactful. I felt overjoyed when they presented me with my certificate. The minister laid hands on my head as I kneeled at the altar, anointed me with oil, and prayed for me. The whole ceremony was unreal to me. How did I get here? Is this for real, or am I dreaming? I stood with the other students from our district and could hardly fathom that I was one of them to receive this high honor from the Lord. We received a towel as a symbol of humility and servanthood. Our Superintendent admonished us from 2 Timothy 4:2 to *"Preach the word; be instant in season, out of season; reprove, rebuke, exhort with all long suffering and doctrine."* I stood in reverential awe and fear of the Lord for what He had done this day in my life. I will remember this day as another great spiritual marker in my journey.

The time had come for me to inform the leadership at my church that I would be leaving to answer the call that God had placed upon my life. It was a joy and privilege for me to serve the Lord as a Pastor. I enjoyed preaching, teaching, and praying with the people of God. It was good to witness spiritual growth in believers, young and old. I believe this must be the greatest joy for a Pastor—to see members of their congregation grow and advance in the things of God and attain spiritual maturity. It was a bittersweet time for me and the church. The leadership was gracious, prayed for me, and released me. It reminded me of when the Lord spoke to me, telling me to leave

Times Square Church because my assignment was completed. They laid hands and prayed for me, then released me.

Similarly, I completed my assignment as Pastor, and it was time for me to move on to the next assignment that the Lord had for me. He had been preparing me for many years for this moment, and it was time to embrace it. In a few weeks, I would preach my last sermon there and then move on in my ministry as an Evangelist.

CHAPTER 15
THE EVANGELIST

Finally, it's here. What I have dreamed of, what God put in my heart as a teenager, what gives me the ultimate joy and fulfillment—preaching the Word and doing the work as an Evangelist. As I accepted the call and stepped out, I would seek the Lord for open doors, the anointing, and His grace to preach. The Lord began to open doors, and I could not be happier. I experience a joy whenever I preach that I cannot explain. It comes from a deep place in my soul. I know it can only come from God. This is where I feel at home—doing what the Lord has called me to do.

Many times, as I drove toward an assignment to preach, I would pray and weep in my car over what the Lord had done. What seemed impossible became possible when I prayed. I cannot emphasize enough the importance of prayer in the life of every believer. God will restore all we lost when we pray. He will even restore the years we lost and help us accomplish for His Kingdom in a short time what would have taken us a lifetime. He said that in His Word, and He will never change His mind or go back on His Word. The more you pray, the more fear will leave you, and God will give you the courage and grace to step out. Amen!

As the Lord opened doors, I would preach at churches on Sunday mornings, Wednesday nights, Friday nights, and Saturdays for women's meetings and conferences. Whatever door the Lord opened, I would answer once I could preach His gospel. As a bi-vocational, I would even take time off from my secular job to preach. My vacation time was all used for ministry. What a joy and great privilege to serve the Lord. To God be the glory! Finally, my heart feels satisfied, but there is much work to be done. There are prayers still to be answered and souls still to be saved.

A few years after I stepped out, COVID-19 came and caused the shutdown of churches. I preached my last message in a church on March 15, 2020. Not only were the churches shut down, but offices were also closed. We began to work from home. This was an interesting time. People were fearful all over the world, as no one was allowed to leave their homes. Parents and children were home together for maybe the first time. Schools were closed. Parents worked from home, and children began to do school online. The world seemed to have just turned upside down.

While our mobility was taken away, it was a great time to get quiet, pray, seek the Lord, study His Word, and spend more time with Him. Either this season would make or break you. Either you would embrace this season or become distraught. It was a time when faith had to conquer fear.

I cannot imagine what this was like for full-time Evangelists who could not go out to preach. I began to seek the Lord as to what I should do. He gave me Psalm 46:10: *"Be still, and know that I am God: I will be exalted among the heathen, I will be exalted in the earth."* I knew exactly what He meant, so I spent much time in prayer and the Word. It was a time for the people of God to take advantage of the quiet and listen to the voice of the Lord. The Scripture is true...

> But as for you, ye thought evil against me; but God meant it unto good, to bring to pass, as it is this day, to save much people alive.
>
> — GENESIS 50:20

God will always turn things around for our good and His glory. We can trust His Word.

After three months, the Lord spoke to me to *"Take the church to the homes."* He began to open up doors to homes, and word got around. There were elderly and bedridden people who could not go to church; I would bring the church to them. Even after some of the restrictions were lifted, some parents did not feel safe taking their little children to church. I took the church to them. This was such a powerful time that many times, the services would go for three or four hours. I normally planned for one and a half to two hours, but sometimes the Holy Spirit would take over when there were hungry hearts. I have seen miracles of healing and salvation. A few times, revival broke out, and family members who had grown cold rededicated their lives to the Lord. At times, joy broke out, and we would dance in the living room, giving praise to God. There were so many testimonies of what the Lord did during this time when the enemy tried to shut the church down. But the church is a living organism, built and established by God, and the Devil or the gates of Hell will never prevail against it.

I remember being contacted by a family member to do a service at a home for a Catholic family. The mom had passed away, and they could not get a priest to come to the house to do a service. It was my joy to bring the hope of Christ to this family. That evening, nine family members gave their lives to Jesus. It was a Wednesday night after work, and on my way back home after the service, I was rejoicing for what the Lord had done. On another occasion, on a Saturday, they asked me to bring the Word at a birthday celebration, and twenty people, mostly young, dedicated their lives to Jesus. This is what gives me joy—seeing people saved, healed, and delivered by the power of God.

As the COVID years seemed to be behind us, the Lord continued to open doors to preach the Word. I still visit a few families and have services every month. The gospel can never be stopped, but we will continue preaching it until Jesus comes again. By whatever means we have to, by whatever door is available, we will preach the good news to a lost and dying world by all means possible.

> And he said unto them, Go ye into all the world, and
> preach the gospel to every creature.
> He that believeth and is baptized shall be saved; but
> he that believeth not shall be damned.
>
> — MARK 16:15-16

This is our mandate!

CHAPTER 16
WHAT NO EYE HAS SEEN

But just as it is written [in Scripture],
"Things which the eye has not seen and the ear has
   not heard,
And which have not entered the heart of man,
All that God has prepared for those who love Him
   [who hold Him in affectionate reverence, who
   obey Him, and who gratefully recognize the benefits that He has bestowed]."

— 1 CORINTHIANS 2:9 (AMP)

None of us can fully grasp all that God has for us until we truly begin to pray. Prayer changes everything—our situation, focus, ministry, calling, life, and even where we live sometimes—everything! Too many believers settle for mediocrity in their walk with the Lord, especially if they have no reference point, role model, or mentor. We've heard the saying "iron sharpens iron," which comes from the wisest king who ever lived, Solomon:

> As iron sharpens iron,
> So one man sharpens [and influences] another
> [through discussion].
>
> — PROVERBS 27:17 (AMP)

> He who walks with wise men will be wise,
> But the companion of fools will be destroyed.
>
> — PROVERBS 13:20 (NKJV)

You may ask, "What if I have no one to help or mentor me?" This was my situation. There was no one to guide or direct me, no spiritual influence except what I heard on the radio from Billy Graham, R. W. Schambach, and what I read in books during my early days. But my hunger was so great that it pushed me into desperate prayer. If all you have is the Bible, the Holy Ghost, and a strong prayer life, then that is enough to cause the Devil to tremble and propel you into destiny.

I did not have a pastor, a church, or anyone around me to call upon or depend on when I was first saved. My church was an outstation that met weekly. In those days, there were no telephones, television, or social media. Getting in touch with my Sunday school teachers before the next Sunday was impossible. This is why my faith in God never depended on others—not that we don't need other believers in our lives, but in the absence of others, you will find that "God alone is enough." Because of this situation, for four years after I was saved, I taught myself how to read the Word, pray, fast, and rely completely on the Lord to answer my prayers. To this day, I very seldom ask for prayer because I learned how to pray and believe God for myself. Part of our spiritual maturity and growth is to know God for ourselves and trust Him. Believers should never remain babes in Christ.

> So that we are no longer children [spiritually immature], tossed back and forth [like ships on a stormy sea] and carried about by every wind of [shifting] doctrine, by the cunning and trickery of [unscrupulous] men, by the deceitful scheming of people ready to do anything [for personal profit].
>
> — EPHESIANS 4:14 (AMP)

We must continue to grow, mature, and stand strong against all the wiles of the Devil. Prayer will help you grow, become strong in the Lord, and experience the power of His might in your life.

Oftentimes, I experienced a spiritual jealousy of ministers who came from a lineage of great Pentecostal men and women of God. I would ask the Lord, "Why didn't I have such a heritage? Why didn't I have grandparents and parents who served the Lord, knew the Holy Spirit, and experienced Pentecost?" The Holy Ghost always reminded me, "It's not by might nor by power, but by My Spirit, says the Lord." He would remind me that it's the same Holy Spirit, and He can do anything in any life that is fully surrendered to Him. When I think of women like Aimee Semple McPherson, Katherine Kuhlman, and Maria Woodworth-Etter, I remind the Lord that I don't have blond hair or blue eyes, but if He can use a nobody—a brunette with brown eyes who came from a poor country and a poor family, with no Pentecostal heritage—then use me. That has been my heart's cry. When I got saved, I felt like our family had a representative in Heaven, one to stand in the gap for them. It has been my prayer that there will be a shift in my family and we will leave a legacy of faith for future generations. God has been faithful, but there are still many more answers to come. Amen!

God is willing to do in and through each one who dares to believe Him more than they can see with the eye or hear with their ears. In Ephesians 3:20, God says He will do more than we can ask or imagine. Can you soak that in for a moment? However big or great you can think in your mind, dream in your dreams, or even imagine, God will do more. This is His word to us. None of us should stop short of His very best for our lives and ministry. D.L. Moody said back in 1873, "The world has yet to see what God will do with a man (or woman) fully consecrated to Him." The world needs you. The world is waiting for you. Each one of us can reach people in our sphere of influence that others cannot. This world not only needs your life and ministry but also depends on them. Don't waste time, but call upon the Lord while He is near; work while it is still day. Live while you are still alive. Amen!

The Bible is full of misfits whom God used greatly to impact their world. Think of these people and see if God cannot use your life greatly: Rahab was a prostitute and became part of the lineage of Jesus. Abraham was an old man who became not only the father of nations but also a friend of God. Joseph faced rejection, abuse, and false accusations, but he eventually became the governor of Egypt. Job lost everything and became bankrupt but kept his faith in God, who restored double to him. Moses could not speak, but he led the Israelites out of Egypt and across the Red Sea. Whether you are a woman or man, young or old, God can use your life to make a difference in this world. Do not procrastinate any longer, but pray yourself out of your current situation and watch God bring you to a place in your natural and spiritual life that you cannot fathom.

One cannot see what God sees through natural sight, but through the eyes of faith, we can catch a glimpse of "what no eye has seen." It's a walk of faith, and as you continue on the journey, God will show you more and more, take you further and further, step by step, and glory to glory. I dare you to step out of your comfort zone and complacency and begin to move forward into the life that God has for you. It will take not only faith but effort on your part to go forth. I am reminded of the four lepers in 2 Kings 7:3-10 who said, "Why sit we here until we die?" The church and society rejected them, but God chose them. Don't wait for someone to help you, pick you up, or mentor you. The Holy Spirit is capable of doing all these things. Begin to call upon the name of the Lord, and you will see changes begin to take place in your life. Do not waste your life; do not sit around and wait to die. Get up, pray, and trust God to make something beautiful of your life. He can take all of your broken pieces and put them together into a vessel of honor for His glory.

Like Moody prayed, the world is yet to see you. With God, it's never too late. He can restore the wasted years, dead dreams, and failures and turn things around that will shock your mind. Whatever the Devil has stolen from you—your future, destiny, ministry, and purpose—God is able to restore. He will not only restore the years but also make everything brand new to the original state that He had for you. Make up your mind that today will be the beginning of a brand-new life. Do not wait for calamity, sickness, or disaster to strike, but do it today while there is breath in your lungs. Too many people wait to turn their lives over to the Lord when bad things happen, and in doing so, they waste many good years. Today is always the best day to come to the Lord and get a new start on life.

When you begin to pray and spend time with the Lord in the Word, your life will begin to change so much that soon you will not recognize yourself. When you look in the mirror, you will not believe it's the same person looking back at you. God will begin to work on you from the inside out, and soon, people around you will notice the difference. Once you have been in the presence of God, you will never be the same. In His presence, we are changed. Prayer changes us. Even when we pray for others or nations, we are changed. This is what the presence of God does when we spend time there. Many believers don't realize the power of prayer. We talk about it, teach about it, preach about it, but don't really believe it because we do not practice it. Anyone who prays will not remain the same. God goes to work on our behalf when we pray. The Devil knows this, and that's why he blocks prayer in our lives. He distracts us with many things and causes us to grow weary. If only the people of God would recognize the power they have when they pray, they would continue 24/7. Prayer shifts the atmosphere in our homes, around us, or wherever we may be. It puts the demonic forces around us to flight. God moves when we pray, things change when we pray, and we change when we pray. Prayer is a power source, and when we lack prayer, we lack the power to live a victorious and overcoming Christian life.

God did not save us or call us to simply get by each day. He called us to live an abundant, prosperous life that reflects His power and glory in us. I never could have imagined what the Lord has done in my life up to this point. I know it's not done yet. It's not over. Greater things He will still do in and through my life. I wish I could get a glimpse of the future and what God has in store for me, but He said, "Trust Me," "Walk by faith," and then you will discover and see. The future is bright when God is leading the way.

In closing this chapter, I must say that it does not matter to God which country you were born in, what your family background or heritage is, what your status in society is, how much money or wealth you have, what your address is, or whether you are rich or poor, learned or unlearned. If God can use a donkey to speak on His behalf, He can most certainly use you and me. The good news is He wants to use you. He is God, and if He called the things that are not into existence, can you begin to imagine what He can do with your life? Only surrender to His will and see what He will do with your life. Nicky Cruz was a murderer and gangster in New York City. As a child, he was given over to the Devil by satanic parents. He was bound for Hell at an accelerated pace. Then God saved him, turned his life around, and he has been preaching the gospel all over the world. They made his life into a movie and wrote books so others could have the same hope and experience the same power of God to change their lives.

Our minds are not capable of comprehending God's mind and all He has in store for the smallest, weakest person who will place their trust in Him. Neither can our eyes see far into the future what He has for each one of us. When God is done putting your life together, it will not only amaze you but also totally marvel and shock you. You will not recognize the old you because now "all things have become new."

CHAPTER 17
LIVE A LIFE OF PURPOSE

The best life to live is to live a life of purpose serving the Lord. The saddest life is a life that is lived without God and merely existing. The Scriptures below show us how much God loves us, thinks about us, cares about us, and the plans He has for each one of us, including you—yes, you! Life is more than just living here on earth and enjoying all that God has created in this world; it is about living for Him. He promised that He came to give us abundant life (John 10:10). What will you gain if you have everything this world can provide and then end up in a lost eternity, forever separated from God? The Bible says you will gain nothing. The abundant life Christ came to give us is not only about enjoying all His blessings in this world but also about being with Him in Heaven when our journey here is over.

Look at these Scriptures below, carefully meditate on each one, and see what God has in mind for you since before you were born. God's plan is not only to bless us but also to fulfill our calling and destiny. You were born with a God-given purpose. Don't leave this world without fulfilling all God has planned.

> For I know the thoughts that I think toward you, saith the Lord, thoughts of peace, and not of evil, to give you an expected end.
> Then shall ye call upon me, and ye shall go and pray unto me, and I will hearken unto you.
> And ye shall seek me, and find me, when ye shall search for me with all your heart.
> And I will be found of you, saith the Lord ...
>
> — JEREMIAH 29:11-14

> For if thou altogether holdest thy peace at this time, then shall there enlargement and deliverance arise to the Jews from another place; but thou and thy father's house shall be destroyed: and who knoweth whether thou art come to the kingdom for such a time as this?
>
> — ESTHER 4:14

> And we know that all things work together for good to them that love God, to them who are the called according to his purpose.
>
> — ROMANS 8:28

> The counsel of the Lord stands forever,
> The thoughts and plans of His heart through all generations.
>
> — PSALM 33:11 (AMP)

"Before I formed you in the womb I knew you [and
 approved of you as My chosen instrument],
And before you were born I consecrated you [to
 Myself as My own];
I have appointed you as a prophet to the nations."

—JEREMIAH 1:5 (AMP)

The Lord does not delay [as though He were unable to act] and is not slow about His promise, as some count slowness, but is [extraordinarily] patient toward you, not wishing for any to perish but for all to come to repentance.

—2 PETER 3:9 (AMP)

I will instruct you and teach you in the way you
 should go;
I will counsel you [who are willing to learn] with My
 eye upon you.

—PSALM 32:8 (AMP)

Trust in the Lord with all thine heart; and lean not
 unto thine own understanding.
In all thy ways acknowledge him, and he shall direct
 thy paths.

—PROVERBS 3:5-6

Did you hear the Spirit speaking to your heart as you read these Scriptures? The Bible contains many more Scriptures that you will discover as you continue to read, read, and read. God is big, and His plans for each one of us are also big. He cannot think small, but it all depends on you and how much you desire to fulfill your full potential. I remember going through some difficult times in life. Many times, the Devil tried to take me out, but God kept me for His purpose. In the difficult times, I cried out to God to bring forth His purpose in my life. I would pray that the reason I was born at this time and season was with purpose, and before I leave this world, I want to fulfill all that God has for me. I know I was born with a purpose and for a purpose.

Satan's whole agenda is to steal your future, destroy your dreams, and kill you if he can. That is why you have been going through so much trouble in this life. He is trying to take you out, but if you are reading this, then he lost, and Jesus won. You are still here, and God did not change His mind about you. He is God, and He changes not (Malachi 3:6). He is the same yesterday, today, and forever. His plans for your life remain the same, and now it's up to you to get up from self-pity and grab hold of them. You may be older now, and you may have wasted many years, but His plan still stands. You may have done everything in ministry, but He has greater things in store for you. Don't despair, for He will use all experiences to mold you to perfection. Nothing goes to waste—whether those around you hurt or betrayed you, God will use it to strengthen you and bring life and hope to others. God will turn around everything the enemy meant to harm you, discourage you, or cause you to give up on Him. What the enemy meant for bad, God will turn around for your good and His glory. Amen!

Too many people buy into the lie of the Devil that they can't do anything for God, that they have no giftings or talents. That's a lie from the Devil. They look at others in ministry and think those people have it all together and are gifted and talented. Most in ministry are people who had nothing, and they will tell you they are nothing outside of God. Some don't know why God even called them into ministry because they have no background or ability in the natural. But God is God, and He makes something out of nothing. He will take you as you are and make something beautiful and honorable of your life. I have known people who did not have an education, never went to school, and did not know how to read or write, but when they came to know Jesus as Lord and Savior and were born again, God, through the Holy Spirit, taught them how to read. Many became pastors and ministers of the gospel. God is not looking for what you have; He is looking for you. Period! Once you surrender to Him, He begins to work out all the kinks in your life and makes you into a vessel of honor for Himself and His glory.

I have seen many talented people who took their talents to the grave and never allowed the Lord to use them in a manner beyond their thinking. The graves are full of untapped gifts and talents that this world never got to enjoy. I implore you to tap into God and let everything He put in you come forth in Jesus' Name! Maybe it's a kind and giving heart; let God use it for His glory. Maybe it's a smile that will bless someone as they walk into a church and see you at the "Welcome Center." Some people can sing, preach, or teach; let the Holy Ghost anoint you. Some can visit the sick in the nursing home; be His hands and feet. We are all called to serve, not just the pastors, evangelists, missionaries, and other ministers. Each one has a Jerusalem, Judea, and Samaria where God can use you to be a light in the darkness and bring the good news of salvation to the lost.

What I have noticed in many people is that they settle for a little when God's promises overflow in every area and aspect of life. Not many churches model prayer that is deep and effective. We see more programs than prayer. God never said that His house should be called a house of programs but a house of prayer. Don't wait on the church; get alone with God, and He will lead you. I created this book out of exactly what I am saying here. I got desperate and began to cry out to God, and He began to do a deeper work in my life. He gave me new desires, new dreams, and new direction. He showed me things and took me to places in the natural and spiritual that I would have never experienced had I not begun to pray.

If there is one thing I am convinced of in this world, it is this: Prayer works. It will change everything. You will come to a place where you don't recognize yourself after being in His presence. He will put a love in your heart for the Word to the point that you will begin to devour it cover to cover like there is not enough. He will give you revelation that you have never seen or heard before. The world will open up to you, and you will see it in a brand-new way and have a new perspective on everything around you. Not only that, but joy and purpose will burst forth. There will be new reasons to jump out of bed in the wee hours of the morning to pray. You will experience a restoration of strength, health, finances, and your smile. His life and light will be reflected in your eyes again, and you will experience a restoration of everything the Devil stole from you, even the years. Hallelujah!

As I close this chapter, I pray that all who read this book will find their God-given purpose for their life and live life to its fullest with God at the center of it all. Purpose in your heart that when your time comes to leave this world, you will say like the Apostle Paul:

> I have fought a good fight, I have finished my course, I have kept the faith:
> Henceforth there is laid up for me a crown of righteousness, which the Lord, the righteous judge, shall give me at that day: and not to me only, but unto all them also that love his appearing.
>
> — 2 TIMOTHY 4:7-8

How beautiful and fulfilling it is to live this life with purpose, serving the Lord, and enjoying all the benefits and blessings that He provides for us here on earth. And when we leave this world, He has rewards that await us. Friends, there is nothing to lose in serving Jesus but all to gain.

> For what is a man profited, if he shall gain the whole world, and lose his own soul? or what shall a man give in exchange for his soul?
>
> — MATTHEW 16:26

CHAPTER 18
FINALLY—IT'S NOT FINISHED YET

> I am convinced and confident of this very thing, that He who has begun a good work in you will [continue to] perfect and complete it until the day of Christ Jesus [the time of His return].
>
> — PHILIPPIANS 1:6 (AMP)

The calling of God on our lives and the work of His Kingdom here on earth will continue until Jesus comes or when we die. I have not yet accomplished everything that the Lord has for me, and I know He still has work for me, and I am not finished yet. The fullness of His calling on my life is still to be attained. So, I press forward toward the mark for the prize of the high calling of God in Christ Jesus (Philippians 3:14).

Since the age of fifteen years old, when I first felt the call as an Evangelist, my prayer has been what Paul wrote to Timothy:

> But as for you, be clear-headed in every situation [stay calm and cool and steady], endure every hardship [without flinching], do the work of an evangelist, fulfill [the duties of] your ministry.
>
> — 2 TIMOTHY 4:5 (AMP)

As each year passes, my desire is to fulfill this call to its fullest and do what the Scriptures say to do:

> "And as you go, preach, saying, 'The kingdom of heaven is at hand.' Heal the sick, raise the dead, cleanse the lepers, cast out demons. Freely you have received, freely give."
>
> — MATTHEW 10:7-8 (AMP)

I believe the best is yet to come, and I look forward to all that God will do in and through my life. I want to flow in the river of God and see a greater manifestation of His power in my generation.

You can also attain all that God has for you. The purpose of writing this book is to show that even the most ordinary and unlikely person can become a giant for God and be used greatly on this earth. It does not matter to God who you are, what you have, or where you live. His plans and purpose for your life remain the same as when you were being formed in your mother's womb. It does not have to be on a mission trip to a foreign country, at some famous Christian conference with great speakers, or at a mega church. Many people cannot afford the cost to even go to these places. Does it mean, then, that God will not use them greatly? Absolutely not!

You could be living now in a barn, a farm, a shed, under a tree—the place does not matter, nor does who you are surrounded by at the moment. This is a time for you and God alone. If you are desperate to be all that you were born to be and fulfill God's calling on your life, then seek Him, cry out to Him, surrender to Him, and watch the transformation begin in your life. Maybe your plans for your life are small and based only on what you have seen or experienced so far. Maybe you don't feel qualified to do anything big for God because of your financial or educational circumstances. If you can get past you and see God, who is big and able to do what is impossible, you can do all He said you can do through the Holy Spirit that works in us who believe.

When the enemy used to bring doubts in my mind about God using me to preach, I would remember how He caused a donkey to speak. If He can cause a donkey to speak, then He can anoint me and use me to speak His Word as well. If He can cause stones to be turned to bread, He can do the impossible for me. If He can call the earth to come forth from nothing, then He can use me to do His bidding. He specializes in doing the impossible. He is God! Remember that!

As you desire to go after God, you will find that the enemy brings all sorts of fears, doubts, and unbelief into your heart. When this happens, just remember God's Word and debunk all of Satan's lies using the sword of the Spirit, which is the Word of God, to put him to flight. Jesus actively used the Word against the Devil when He was tempted. Whatever happens, keep going forward—don't look back, don't look left or right, and don't look at other people—but set your eyes like a flint and go hard after God. You will see the results and change in your life. Greater things await you!

I found it astonishing that despite being a Christian for about twenty-four years, I had such limited knowledge of God and minimal experience with Him. I loved the Lord and served Him in a role I was accustomed to and felt at ease in, specifically within children and youth ministry. I never thought, desired, or dreamed of anything more. I never felt qualified or good enough. Everything changed when I encountered the Lord in a life-changing way in prayer at my kitchen table. Prayer was birthed in me that night, and I sensed Heaven opening over my life, signaling imminent change. I was on a path pursuing God in desperate prayer as never before, and nothing could stop me. I touched something of God that I never did before, and I was not about to let it go. The whole world seemed to be at my disposal, and I was not worried or fearful anymore.

Soon, people began to notice things in me that I never thought about or realized. I remember traveling and talking to the passenger next to me on the plane, and they asked if I was a Minister. I would say no, I am just a Christian. I remember when people began to call me their Pastor long before I ever was one. Many times, while traveling in a train, taxi, or plane, I would share the gospel and lead people to salvation in Christ. They would ask if I was a Minister or Pastor, and I would always say, "No, I am just a Christian." As you spend time in prayer, you will find that God will begin work in your heart, and people will notice and call you out. Pay attention to what people are saying about you. Maybe they are seeing what God is about to birth in you, but you can't see it yet.

Once at Times Square Church, I walked past a woman, and the anointing on me hit her. She grabbed me and asked me to pray for her. This has happened many times in different places. You will hear prophetic words from people over your life. Listen, keep it in your heart, and bring it to the Lord in prayer. Not everything you hear "prophetically" is from God—test the spirit to see if it lines up with the Word and what you already know in your heart. Many times, it's a confirmation of what you already know and what God has placed in your heart. A prophetic word will always encourage you and align with the Word of the Lord and the Spirit of God in you.

I am cautious about who lays hands on me. I am very careful of that. If I don't know you and your walk with God, I will not allow you to lay your hands on me. I believe it's my right to say no to anyone who shows up in a church and wants to pray or lay hands on me. I appreciate men and women who are anointed by God and bear the fruits of the Spirit laying hands on me. As a matter of fact, I seek those out whose anointing I desire to be imparted to me by the laying on of hands.

A few times, I have had people walk up to me at church events and meetings and prophesy about "a book" I should be writing. There was a time when a Minister walked up to me and said, "When will you start writing that book?" I smiled because I knew that God had spoken to me to write this book, but I did not sense the direction it should go, so I decided to put it off. I wondered if she just said that to me, if she gives that same word to many others, or if she actually heard from the Lord. There is always a question when you hear a word like this. You must know and discern what is of God and what is not. Many prophets out there give "a word" that will make you feel good, so be wary of the schemes of the Devil. Know who you are in Christ, stand on the Word, and do not deviate from it—not for anyone or anything. Amen!

AFTERWORD

A few months after the Lord spoke to me about writing this book, He exploded the revelation of Matthew 6:33 in my heart:

> But seek ye first the kingdom of God, and his righteousness; and all these things shall be added unto you.

The NLT states, "Make God your primary concern." This changed my life; if I give God first place, seeking Him above all, He will accomplish more in and through me than I can ask or imagine. He will do this for you too!

Do not settle where you are now. Believe God, trust Him, and then watch Him take you from nothing to something the world needs.

Now is the time to rise up and run hard after God. Leave everything and everyone in your dust. Do not look back, but set your eyes like a flint and go hard. You will not regret it.

See you on the other side!

About the Author

Jessica Seetaram was born and raised in British Guyana, South America, and was the first in her family to come to faith in Jesus Christ. Saved at fifteen, she has been a lifelong Pentecostal, passionate about revival, and hopeful for America's last great awakening. Over the years, Jessica has served in many capacities, including twenty-four years as a Sunday School teacher, Women's Bible Study Leader, Director of Prayer Ministry, CA Secretary, pastor, and evangelist. Her ministry began on the streets, where she discovered her love for outdoor preaching—a preference she holds to this day. A graduate of the City University of New York with a BS in Accounting and Literature, Jessica has worked over thirty years in banking. She completed her Bible studies at the New York District School of Ministry in 2015 and was ordained by the Assemblies of God in 2017. Today, Jessica's life and ministry continue to be a powerful testament to the impact of prayer, fasting, and a hunger for God's presence, inspiring others to seek the Lord wholeheartedly and embrace His call.